Walks, Walls & Patios

PLAN ▪ DESIGN ▪ BUILD

Walks, Walls & Patios

PLAN ▪ DESIGN ▪ BUILD

CREATIVE HOMEOWNER®, Upper Saddle River, New Jersey

VP/Editorial Director: Timothy O. Bakke
Production Manager: Kimberly H. Vivas

Senior Editor: Fran J. Donegan
Photo Editor/Assistant Editor: Jennifer Ramcke
Editorial Assistant: Jennifer Doolittle
Indexer: Schroeder Indexing Services

Art Direction/Design: Glee Barre
Illustrations: Ron Carboni, Craig Franklin,
    Paul M. Schumm
Illustration Enhancements: Clarke Barre
Cover Design: Glee Barre

Manufactured in the United States of America

Current Printing (last digit)
10 9 8 7 6 5 4 3 2

Walks, Walls & Patios
Library of Congress Catalog Card Number:
2002104988
ISBN: 1-58011-095-9

CREATIVE HOMEOWNER®
A Division of Federal Marketing Corp.
24 Park Way, Upper Saddle River, NJ 07458
www.creativehomeowner.com

Safety

Although the methods in this book have been reviewed for safety, it is not possible to overstate the importance of using the safest methods you can. What follows are reminders—some do's and don'ts of work safety—to use along with your common sense.

■ Always use caution, care, and good judgment when following the procedures described in this book.

■ Always be sure that the electrical setup is safe, that no circuit is overloaded, and that all power tools and outlets are properly grounded. Do not use power tools in wet locations.

■ Always read container labels on paints, solvents, and other products; provide ventilation; and observe all other warnings.

■ Always read the manufacturer's instructions for using a tool, especially the warnings.

■ Use hold-downs and push sticks whenever possible when working on a table saw. Avoid working short pieces if you can.

■ Always remove the key from any drill chuck (portable or press) before starting the drill.

■ Always pay deliberate attention to how a tool works so that you can avoid being injured.

■ Always know the limitations of your tools. Do not try to force them to do what they were not designed to do.

■ Always check that any adjustment is locked before proceeding. For example, always check the rip fence on a table saw or the bevel adjustment on a portable saw before starting work.

■ Always clamp small pieces to a bench or other work surface when using a power tool.

■ Always wear the appropriate rubber gloves or work gloves when handling chemicals, moving or stacking lumber, working with concrete, or doing heavy construction.

■ Always wear a disposable face mask when you create dust by sawing or sanding. Use a special filtering respirator when working with toxic substances and solvents.

■ Always wear eye protection, especially when using power tools or striking metal on metal or concrete; a chip can fly off, for example, when chiseling concrete.

■ Never work while wearing loose clothing, open cuffs, or jewelry; tie back long hair.

■ Always be aware that there is seldom enough time for your body's reflexes to save you from injury from a power tool in a dangerous situation; everything happens too fast. Be alert!

■ Always keep your hands away from the business ends of blades, cutters, and bits.

■ Always hold a circular saw firmly, usually with both hands.

■ Always use a drill with an auxiliary handle to control the torque when using large-size bits.

■ Always check your local building codes when planning new construction. The codes are intended to protect public safety and should be observed to the letter.

■ Never work with power tools when you are tired or when under the influence of alcohol or drugs.

■ Never cut tiny pieces of wood, vinyl, metal, or pipe using a power saw. When you need a smaller piece, saw it from a securely clamped longer piece.

■ Never change a saw blade or a drill or router bit unless the power cord is unplugged. Do not depend on the switch being off. You might accidentally hit it.

■ Never work in insufficient lighting.

■ Never work with dull tools. Have them sharpened, or learn how to sharpen them yourself.

■ Never use a power tool on a workpiece—large or small—that is not firmly supported.

■ Never saw a workpiece that spans a large distance between horses without close support on each side of the cut; the piece can bend, closing on and jamming the blade, causing saw kickback.

■ When sawing, never support a workpiece from underneath with your leg or any other part of your body.

■ Never carry sharp or pointed tools or materials, such as utility knives, awls, or chisels, in your pocket. If you want to conveniently carry any of these tools, use a special-purpose tool belt that has leather pockets and holders.

Contents

Introduction

alks, walls, and patios turn outdoor areas into usable living spaces. Walks connect the focal points of your yard, both physically and visually. A brick, stone, or block wall adds character and privacy. A patio links your house and yard, providing outdoor living, eating, cooking, and entertainment spaces.

This book will help you get started creating these structures for your yard. An extensive design section aids in laying out your property and planning your project. The section also deals with the practical matters of drainage, and sun and climate control.

The rest of the book is devoted to helping you design and build the projects that will increase the value of your home and make your yard more livable. Grouped into sections that cover walks, walls, and patios, each chapter covers a specific type of structure. Each section contains dozens of design ideas that you can use in your own yard. The projects themselves are the most popular among homeowners and designers. The materials and tools needed to complete them are readily available. The instructions provided here are simple and straightforward. Each sequence lists the tools and materials you will need to do the job and easy-to-follow directions for completing the projects.

Opposite *Brick is one of the most popular building materials used for constructing walks, walls, and patios.*

Above *Building a dry-laid stone wall, even a retaining wall, is a good project for the do-it-yourselfer.*

Below *Many patio materials, including natural stone, are installed on a sand-and-gravel base without mortar.*

Planning and Design

Gallery of Design Ideas

1 Begin planning your patio by thinking about how the area will be used. For relaxing in the sun as shown here, any open, well-drained spot in the yard will work fine.

2 This curving brick walk and the plantings that flank it turn what would otherwise be a wasted space into a garden focal point.

3 Walls provide privacy and architectural detail, but they also serve as the backdrop for garden accents and climbing plants.

4 New walkways, and walls and patios for that matter, should appear as though they were always a part of your yard's landscape.

5 This area contains a brick patio, privacy wall, and low, open wall of a different design. Note how the pilasters on the large wall create design interest; the white cap stones tie the two walls together.

6 These stepping stones set in the lawn not only provide a walkway from one part of the yard to another, they also help define the planting bed along side of the building.

Gallery of Design Ideas

1 To complete an area, combine patios with overhead structures and fences.

2 Combining different walkway materials can help signal a transition from one area to another.

3 Although permanent, mortared-stone walls and patios work well in an informal landscape design.

4 Stone steps should follow the natural contours of the slope they climb.

5 The change in level and the imposing pillars signal a change in intended use for these two patio areas.

6 Few landscape elements are as appealing as a stone wall overgrown with flowering plants.

7 The formality of the stone wall and patio is softened by the container plants, garden accents, and casual furniture.

Basic Landscape Design

What Do You Expect From Your Yard?

Basic Site Design

Good landscape design requires a blend of elements. It involves combining technical considerations, which are dictated by the site and your budget, and creative possibilities. In landscape design, especially when it comes to hardscapes such as walks, walls, and patios, each site is unique and offers its own challenges. But there are basic principles you can follow to create a design that best meets the needs of you and your family.

Site design and planning complete your yard. A well-designed site extends your house beyond the walls and helps to bring your daily life into contact with the outdoors. The benefits to you can be substantial and rewarding. By taking the time to understand a few basic principles about designing a site, you will be able to create an outdoor area that is more comfortable and relaxing; more private and secure; warmer in the winter and cooler in the summer; and, well, just more pleasant and satisfying to you, your family, and your friends.

tors for you to consider as you begin the design process:

Identifying. Your first order of business should be recognizing the unique combination of elements that your site has to offer. These could be such things as special views and vistas; natural features such as trees, rocks, or streams; or even historical artifacts or events that occurred there in the past. Any and all of these will add up to the unique spirit of your particular location. Spend some time getting acquainted with your landscape and noting these special features. Every site has something to tell you—you just need to listen to what it has to say.

Intensifying. Once you feel that you understand the special qualities and elements of your site, think of ways in which these features can be preserved and, better yet, enhanced through the placement of such things as walks, walls, patios, and vegetation.

What Do You Expect From Your Yard?

In many ways, the concept of site design goes back a long time. The Romans called it **genius loci**—spirit of place. When designed correctly, a place affects all of our senses by providing a combination of sights, sounds, smells, textures, and temperatures. A place is memorable; we can return to it again and again in our minds whenever we want. We all have special places that we hold dear. A good site design can and should provide a memorable experience for all who visit that particular place. Essentially, there are two fac-

Above Work with your site, not against it. The owners of the property above chose to enhance their sloping yard by installing the stone retaining wall.

Right The radiating circular pattern of this patio helps establish the presence of this small area within the larger yard.

Left Sometimes a simple design is the best solution. Here a winding gravel path bordered with loose stones connects one part of the yard with another.

WORKING WITH YOUR SURROUNDINGS

If your site is in a historic district or in an architecturally distinct region of the country—New England or the Southwest come to mind—your design will fit into these contexts if you make an effort to work with the prevailing materials, colors, and architectural elements. This doesn't necessarily mean copying or mimicking every little detail you can find in your neighborhood. There's still plenty of latitude here to design your personal interpretation of what you think makes your region or neighborhood unique. Of course, the choice of whether or not you want to fit into or stand out from your surroundings is entirely up to you. In fact, with so many of today's newer houses looking pretty much like duplicates of every other house in the neighborhood, this is the perfect opportunity to express your personal values and tastes.

Opposite Although the design appears formal in style, the choice of materials for the walk and plantings give this garden setting an organic feel.

Above This straight path leads to a garden destination, and it helps anchor the plantings that flank the path.

Right Flat stones set in an informal way appear as if they have always been part of the site.

One design concept popular in landscape planning involves creating designs that are "of the site" versus those that are not. A design that is considered of the site appears to grow or spring directly from what is already a part of the site, as if the new design were always meant to be there. Frank Lloyd Wright liked to call this "organic design."

Imported Designs. The opposite of an "of the site" design is one that seems to be imported or brought to the site form somewhere else, such as a New England Cape Cod house plopped down in the middle of the Sonora Desert. Although most professional site designers prefer the more organic approach, that doesn't mean you can't incorporate something like a Japanese Zen rock and sand garden into your design if you wish. It simply means being sensitive and not trying to force something onto the site that seems unnatural or incongruous. As with much of site design (particularly when dealing with drainage!), the best advice is to work with the site and not against it.

FORMAL VERSUS INFORMAL

Consider whether you want a formal layout; a more relaxed, informal layout; or some combination of both. Consider the size and shape of your lot, the style of the house itself, and your lifestyle needs and preferences. Formal site layouts are usually symmetrical and uniform, whereas informal site layouts are typically asymmetrical with irregular or naturally flowing shapes. Feel free to mix formal and informal layouts in your overall design; some of the most satisfying site plans have aspects of both.

By combining both informal and formal elements in close proximity, each will enhance and strengthen both through their obvious contrasts. For example, you might try a formal patio layout integrated into a system of informal, curvilinear walks, walls, and planting areas. But remember that informal doesn't mean random or chaotic. An underlying sense of balance is just as important to informal layouts as it is to formal layouts. Base a curving walk or wall on circles, radii, and tangents, not just careless squiggles across your site.

Enclosure. The best site designs provide varying degrees of enclosure. A good way to think of enclosure is in terms of shelter—how much we are protected from the elements and how much the enclosure provides a sense of privacy and intimacy. A sense of enclosure or positive space is really very simple to achieve, but it certainly does not mean an airtight box. After all, you want to be outdoors to enjoy a free, open feeling. To achieve a satisfying degree of enclosure, a low wall along the edge of a planting area or along the side of a walk—even the edge of a patio with one or more low planters—is all you need.

A Sense of Security. Perhaps you remember how pleasant and secure it felt to sit on the front porch of your grandparents' house in the summertime, or perhaps you have another special place that gave you a feeling of security. Ever wish you could re-create that feeling? Well, you can. The people who study these types of things say that humans have a natural tendency to seek slightly elevated and sheltered places and to avoid open, exposed places whenever possible. The slight elevation allows you to see farther in all directions, and the semi-open shelter provides you with a sense of security and allows you to watch and participate in the passing world. Whether it's in your front or backyard, you can create this sense of security by elevating your patio slightly above the surrounding grade, providing a sense of enclosure with a few low walls and planters, and perhaps adding an overhead trellis or patio roof to provide shade and rain protection. Voilà! Time to make some lemonade.

Outdoor Scale. A quick note about outdoor scale versus indoor scale. No rocket science here, folks. Outdoor spaces need to be scaled up from the typical dimensions used for rooms inside. If you are using an average-size room inside your house to get a feel for the size of your new patio, add a few extra feet to the dimensions, if possible. What seems like a perfectly adequate space inside can feel uncomfortably cramped and small when it is outside. And

Positive and Negative Spaces. Site designers often talk about creating positive and negative spaces. This is a simple yet extremely important aspect of designing a good site. Positive space refers to well-defined and enclosed spaces, while negative space refers to poorly defined spaces and/or spaces with little or no sense of enclosure. Think of trying to drink out of a good, solid coffee mug versus a sieve or of keeping your valuables in a good, solid safe versus a paper bag. Positive spaces, with well-defined borders and edges—walls or walkways, for example—help to gather and contain as well as define spaces. They have a feeling of reaching around and embracing you. Negative spaces, on the other hand, tend to leak and flow out and away from you. As human beings we tend to find negative or shapeless spaces much less satisfying than well-defined, positive spaces.

you thought you weren't going to get a good reason for making that new patio just a little bit larger!

Forcing Perspective. Here are a couple of neat tricks to use when working with small spaces. The perceived size of a space can be increased by slightly narrowing the far end of the area in relation to the width of the end nearest the viewer. This is called forced perspective, and it is a trick that landscape designers learned from painters. It works because our eyes trick our brains into thinking that the space is longer than it really is. Create this type of perspective by placing larger or taller trees or shrubs in the foreground of a space and then placing smaller, shorter trees or shrubs toward the far end of the space.

Opposite This wall provides a sense of security, but the plants and picket fence soften the overall design.

Above The low wall and surrounding plantings serve to give this patio a sense of enclosure.

Below Even a slight elevation makes a patio feel more comfortable and inviting.

Varying Texture. Use fine and coarse textures to increase (or decrease) your perception of spatial depth. Think about standing on a small mountaintop and looking out into the distance. We can see every leaf on the trees and shrubs near us. Then as we look farther out into the distance, the leaves begin to blur until we can no longer perceive individual leaves or even individual trees. By varying the textures of the vegetation and/or the wall surfaces in small spaces from coarse at the near end to finely textured at the far end, you can trick your eyes into thinking that the space is larger than it really is. The reverse is also true (just in case you want to make a large space look smaller).

OTHER PLANNING CONSIDERATIONS

Here are a few additional points to consider as you attempt to find the right site for your project.

Site Repair. Use this opportunity to fix up the neglected area. Rather than picking the nicest

spot in your backyard to locate your new patio or other site improvements, choose an area that could stand some enhancement or repair.

Maintenance. It goes without saying that maintenance is an important consideration, especially outdoors. Once your new patio and walks are constructed, it's time to take care of them. Obviously, it pays to select durable and easily cleaned materials, but keep in mind that your design can also create headaches when it comes to cleaning, raking, sweeping, shoveling snow, etc. Odd angles and tight corners might increase your cleaning tasks. If you live in snow country, ask yourself where you will pile the snow from your walks and patio, and plan accordingly.

Life-Cycle Costs. Over the long run, the cheapest materials may turn out to be the most expensive if they need to be replaced or repaired often. For example, if you have 100 square feet of a material that costs $3.00 per square foot and it needs to be

totally replaced every five years, the annual replacement cost will be $60.00 (100 square feet x $3.00 = $300.00 divided by 5 years). On the other hand, if you pick a material that costs $4.50 per square foot and it needs to be replaced every ten years, the annual replacement cost will only be $45.00 (100 square feet x $4.50 = $450.00 divided by 10 years). Balance initial costs with long-term replacement and maintenance costs when designing a project.

Basic Site Design

To get to the point where you can put your ideas onto a site drawing, you will first have to understand some basic techniques and terms. Don't worry if you don't grasp the terms immediately. Read through the next section before attempting a design. As you work on your plan, you will find that terms and ideas will become apparent to you.

smart tip

STEAL SOME IDEAS
Don't be afraid to borrow ideas and designs from friends and neighbors. Most people find it flattering when someone copies them. It is also a good way for you to learn about potential maintenance problems and long-term life-cycle costs.

Left *The symmetry of this straight path balances with the asymmetrical appearance of the plantings.*

Above *The casual winding path tempers the severe look of the low stone wall.*

DESIGN TECHNIQUES

These basic design techniques are more or less common to all design professions including artists.

Balance. You should arrange various site elements so that they are resolved and balanced. Think of a fulcrum or teeter-totter as you attempt to balance the elements. A visually heavy or larger object can be balanced by a lighter or smaller object in the site if the smaller object is darker in color value, is unusually or irregularly shaped, has a contrasting texture, or is more elaborately detailed.

All of these strategies will help to draw attention to the smaller object and thereby visually balance it with the larger object. For example, let's say you have a large clump of conifer trees on one side of your yard. To visually balance the trees you might plant smaller, more colorful ornamental trees on the other side of the yard, or you might install a manmade object such as a decorative fountain or a gazebo to balance the large trees.

Harmony. Harmony can be achieved by selecting and using elements that share a common trait or characteristic. By using elements that are similar in size, shape, color, material, texture, or detail, you can create a cohesive feeling and relation among the various elements on the site. An example of this might be a brick patio that is bordered by a brick planter near a brick walkway leading to a brick-lined garden area. In this case, the various elements are made of a common material. Another example might be using a common shape, such as a square. Imagine having a square concrete patio scored in a square (or diamond) pattern with a square table, square chairs, and a square-checkered tablecloth. The results can be extremely pleasing.

Unity and Variety. While both balance and harmony are used to achieve unity, too much unity can be boring. That's where variety and contrast come in handy. By varying size, shape, color, material, texture, and detail, you can introduce a note of interest or a focal point into the total composition. For instance, placing a round wooden planter onto the square-patterned patio discussed earlier will provide a pleasing contrast of both shape and material. The contrasting object (the round wooden planter) will draw attention to itself and provide a degree of visual relief and interest to the total setting. This is the right time and place to add your individual touch, including a bit of whimsy or humor if that feels right. However, too much variety can be worse than too much unity and result in a confusing, chaotic jumble. When introducing variety into your plan layout, it's probably better to lean toward the conservative side.

Rhythm. In design terms, rhythm—or the spacing of elements relative to similar elements—can create another type of unity in a composition. Rhythm helps to establish a visually satisfying progression or sequence to a site design. For example, on a walkway, you can establish a regular rhythm if you place a band of decorative brick at 4-foot intervals. This acts as both a control joint and as a source of visual rhythm. Or as another example, you can place pilasters or half-columns along a brick or masonry wall at regular intervals.

On the other hand, a song composed of only one sequence of notes is boring. You can avoid visual boredom by varying such things as the interval, color, size, shape, texture, or material of the elements you use to create your sequence. Another fun way to introduce an interesting visual rhythm is to create subsets of elements between the evenly spaced elements. Between the regularly spaced pilasters of the brick or masonry wall in the example above, you could place a series of colorful glazed tiles with their own rhythmic sequence.

Opposite The natural colors of the flagstone give the walk a lively, interesting look.

Left This narrow path opens to a highly stylized stairs and landing.

Right Choosing materials of similar colors creates a unified design.

Emphasis. A lot like unity and variety, emphasis assumes that within your site some of the elements have more significance or importance than the rest and that these special elements should be somehow identified as such. You can emphasize an element in any one of a number of ways, including making it larger than other elements, placing it among items that have a different shape, centering it within a circle or at the end of a walkway, or highlighting it at night with floodlights or accent lights. But as with unity and variety, if you emphasize everything then nothing is really emphasized and you end up with a chaotic, visually confusing site design. Use this one with caution.

Simplicity. Don't be fooled. Just because simplicity is the last item on the list doesn't mean it's the least important. In fact, to many design-ers it's probably the most important concept of all—and you thought this was going to be complicated! Ironically, simplicity is also one of the hardest things to achieve in any design concept. That's because when you realize how many design tools and elements you have to work with, you have a natural tendency to want to use all of them.

Remember trying to mix every color in your new watercolor set together just to see what that color would look like? Remember the results? In virtually every case, the most elegant and satisfying site designs are those that begin and end with simplicity as a guiding design principle. The Zen rock gardens of Japan are perhaps the best example of this way of designing—so much is said with so little effort. And that's probably because so much is left to our own individual interpretations. Subtlety and simplicity are good words to remember.

DIVIDING YOUR DESIGN INTO SPECIFIC PARTS

There is more to a design, however, than the actual physical parts and conceptual places of any given site. To help you arrive at your overall plan, you will have to juggle the following design elements.

Centers. Centers are gathering areas where people come together for a common purpose. We are typically drawn to centers because of their location or placement on the site and their sense of importance within the design. On a larger scale, some examples of centers might be the town square in a traditional New England village or even Rockefeller Center in New York. For our purposes, the obvious example of a center is the patio you are about to design. What are some of the social activities you intend to accommodate in your new patio?

Opposite *This low wall and straight slate path contribute to an elegant design. The stone borders around the plantings separate them from the gravel area.*

Above *Knowing how your patio will be used will help you create a useful design. For this patio, site selection was one its most important elements.*

smart tip

PLAN FOR THE FUTURE
The ways in which you use your new patio will help determine its value. Don't forget to add some amenities, such as a lighting system, an outdoor electrical receptacle, space for a grill, storage for patio furniture, and room to add a spa or hot tub later.

Above Some boundaries carry more weight than others. In addition to being a safety feature, this fence visually separates a raised patio from the rest of the yard.

Below When creating your landscape, use walls and paths to create districts within your yard. Here low walls separate lawn and patio areas.

Edges. Edges can be thought of as the linear boundaries between distinctly different areas. Edges can take many forms: natural features, such as streams and rows of shrubs, or man-made elements, such as walls. Low walls, such as the ones illustrated in this book, provide very effective edges that separate areas in a yard, such as planting beds and lawns. Edges give these areas a crisp definition that is much more aesthetically pleasing than unclear, poorly defined boundaries.

Districts. Districts can also be thought of as areas, zones, or fields. For our purposes, examples of districts might include lawn areas, flower beds, play areas, gardens, and especially patios.

Paths. Paths are the obvious complements to the areas of your site. Paths or, better yet, walks connect the outdoor rooms of your site together and make them usable and accessible, and therefore deserve a high degree of thought and consideration on your part.

Nodes. Nodes are basically the same as centers, except that they are more closely associated with walks. You might also think of them as intersections or crossroads. Because intersections are typically busy places when there is a lot of traffic, consider enlarging the major nodes or intersections of your site plan to accommodate passing room or the occasional impromptu conversation.

ORGANIZING YOUR SITE DESIGN

So how are you going to organize all the elements of your site? That's where the use of one or more ordering systems can help make sense of it all. These are the planning tools we can use to gather and arrange the physical places of your site into a cohesive, unified whole instead of a haphazard assortment of unrelated spaces.

Keep in mind, though, that using an ordering system doesn't exclude variety, spontaneity, and points of emphasis within your plan. Also, you might consider using more than one ordering system, depending on which element or place you're designing. For example, a grid system might work best when you are laying out the walls for a lawn and garden area; then you might switch to a symmetrical layout for the patio and to an axial layout for the walks. Impress your friends and neighbors, not to mention your family. Let's see what's in the planning toolbox.

Axes. An axis is an imaginary yet powerful line. You can arrange your outdoor rooms or the lineal elements such as walks and walls on either side of an axis to achieve a sense of balance. An axis will end either in a panoramic view or with a symmetrical vertical element such as a statue, fountain, or arbor. Walks and sight lines are good places to use an axial layout.

Grids. Grids can be useful in site design. For example, you might think of your yard as a nine-square grid. When planning your layout, you might overlay this grid on your site to organize such elements as patios, play areas, gardens, and a gazebo. In arranging elements in your grid, consider such factors as traffic patterns, views, and the path of the sun over the yard.

Above Try to incorporate both horizontal and vertical elements. This walk forms an axis within this setting that leads to the statue in the background.

Below All roads lead somewhere. Here a collection of short paths flanked by flower and shrub beds empty into a larger patio.

emphasize plantings of various shapes. Interestingly enough, grids also make good datum lines, as when you overlay a variety of differently shaped objects on a regular pattern. The grid holds everything together.

Basic Geometry. Geometric shapes are always fun to use when designing just about anything, especially site plans. The basic geometric shapes are the circle, square, and triangle. With these shapes, combined with the other ordering systems, you can design just about everything that comes along. Interesting geometric variations include overlapping the basic shapes to form a third shape (or space) and creating spiral or pinwheel compositions. All of these geometric systems can be combined, overlapped, rotated, and shifted relative to each other and themselves for added variety and complexity. In your yard, the geometric elements might be a triangular trellis, rectangular patios, and round shrubs.

Hierarchy. You will use hierarchy to rank spaces and elements by order of importance. Every site plan has certain spaces that are more important than others. Think of it this way: normally, the living room is a far more important space than the utility room. You put your best furnishings and carpets and the most money into the living room—not the utility room. Your priorities are up to you, but it's a good bet that your new patio is probably going to be the most important space you are planning.

You can give your important spaces the amount of attention they deserve by making them larger than the other spaces, by giving them an unusual or unique shape (for example, a round space within a square grid), or by locating the space in a prominent position, such as the center of your site or at the end of an axis.

Datum. A datum is a reference point, or more accurately, a reference line or plane. An axis is a datum in that it gives elements on either side of it a common line of reference. Walls make good datum lines. Their presence and continuity often help emphasize unique elements. For example, a fence could act as a datum to

Opposite top *When viewed from above, the gridlike appearance of the patio tiles gives this area a neat and ordered appearance.*

Opposite bottom *This arbor acts as a datum line in this design as it emphasizes the curves of the patio and low boundary wall.*

Right *Geometric shapes play a large role in this design. Note how the grid of the shade structure filters the sunlight.*

Below *Some design elements are more important than others. While the slate patio is important, the pillars give the porch more prominence in the overall scheme.*

2

Planning Your Site

Dealing with Drainage

Creating a
Comfortable Climate
for Your Patio

Walks

Designing Your Site

Making a Site Plan

Before you can actually apply the design principles covered in the previous chapter, you need to familiarize yourself with some of the more mundane, yet important, aspects of landscape design. Such things as the soil, drainage patterns, and grading are extremely important for your final design. After all, even the most beautiful patio won't be very pleasant to use if it is under several inches of water. The most carefully laid out walks won't function if they turn into rivers of mud when it rains, and the retaining wall you're thinking of putting in won't serve its purpose very well if it cracks or falls over.

Types of Soil

Soils have three main properties that we are interested in: the bearing (structural) capacity, the drainage characteristics, and the fertility (ability to support plant life). Soils are divided into two major classifications, depending on the size of the soil particles. There are coarse-grained soils, such as gravel and sand, and fine-grained soils, such as clays and silts.

For both structural and drainage purposes, the coarse-grained soils

are preferable. As you can imagine, coarse-grained soils will support more weight and will drain much better than fine-grained soils. Soils such as clays and stilts, besides having poor structural and drainage capacities, also have a tendency to expand as they become saturated with ground water and then shrink as they dry out. This can cause major problems such as cracking and excessive settling of walks, patios, and footings. If you suspect that the soil on your site has these characteristics, you should remove it to a suitable depth and replace it with coarser soil.

Almost every county in the United States has a County Soil Conservation Service, which will provide countywide soil surveys, indicating the predominant soil types in your area. Another source for this information is your local plant nursery, which will have a general knowledge of soil types in your community.

smart tip

GOOD FOUNDATIONS
Be sure to include a 4-to 6-inch layer of gravel under your patio and walkways. The gravel acts as a drainage system that keeps water from collecting or ponding beneath these shallow constructions.

DRAINAGE SYSTEMS

Uphill

Downhill

Swale directs water away from house.

Berm directs water away from house.

Swale collects water and carries it to a lower site.

Above *Natural slopes help carry water away from the house. Here a swale at the bottom of the short incline diverts water to a lower area in the yard and away from the house and the stone walkway.*

Dealing with Drainage

Unless you happen to live on a rock in the middle of the Mojave Desert, you probably already know where the low spots on your site are. You know the locations of those miniature bogs and swamps where the water tends to collect after every good rain. Note and record these places, as well as the existing natural drainage patterns, on your site plan. Here is your opportunity to correct any annoying drainage problems you may find on your property.

However, the best advice is to identify and work with the natural drainage paths whenever possible. (See "Drainage Systems," opposite.) These existing paths have generally reached a state of equilibrium with the surrounding terrain. Altering, blocking, or interfering with these natural paths requires expert planning, extra labor, and materials—and can be disastrous if not done properly.

DRAINAGE SYSTEMS

Site drainage involves the collection of rainwater and snow runoff, the channeling of this water, and the disposal of the excess water. There are two primary kinds of systems: surface drain systems and subsurface drain systems, such as area drains, catch basins, trench drains, dry wells, and drain tiles. Due to the expense and work involved, use subsurface systems only as a last resort.

Surface drain systems basically consist of shallow drainage ditches, called swales, and built-up mounds that direct runoff, called berms. After you have identified where runoff enters your site, the next step is to decide where to channel this water. Generally, you'll want to direct it to an existing storm sewer located in the street. You'll try to channel this water with swales, berms, and retaining walls. If for any reason it is impossible to run storm water to the street system, a substitute location must be chosen (and, no, not in your neighbor's yard). The new drainage pattern should not cause damage to or increase runoff to surrounding properties.

GRADING YOUR SITE

Site grading involves reshaping and recontouring the earth, which is a fancy way of saying "moving a lot of dirt around." Try to work with the existing contours whenever possible to minimize time and expenses. The grading operation consists of two basic operations: cutting and filling. A cut involves removing dirt (that is, cutting into a hillside), and a fill involves adding dirt to the original grade. To avoid having to move excess dirt to or from your site, try to balance the amount of dirt you wish to cut with the amount you wish to fill.

Choosing the Right Slope. Site grading accomplishes two things. The first is functional and involves creating relatively flat areas and walks. The second enhances the aesthetic and sensory qualities of the site. Remember that a completely flat area can be just as undesirable as an excessively steep slope. Water will inevitably collect and remain in a flat area. For this reason, provide a slight slope to play areas, patios, and other areas of use. What we are really trying to do is to find a balance between creating relatively flat areas and avoiding water incursion and ponding. Recommended maximum and minimum slopes for different areas are shown in "Suggested Slopes for Good Drainage," below. Note that a 0 percent slope is never recommended.

Suggested Slopes for Good Drainage

To determine the percentage of your existing or proposed slopes, simply divide the vertical distance or drop by the horizontal distance (run). For example, a slope that drops 2 feet in 25 feet of run would be equal to an 8 percent slope (2 / 25 = 0.08, or 8 percent).

Here are some recommended slopes for various areas:

	Minimun	Maximum
Walkways, Approaches, and Entrances	0.5%	5%
Patios	1%	2%
Lawn and play areas	0.5%	4%
Swales	1%	10%
Grassy Banks		25%
Planted Banks (vines or groundcover)		50%

Right No patio or walk should be dead level. They all should have a slight slope to aid in surface drainage.

Below In most cases, you can improve the drainage on your property by working with the existing topography and installing berms and retaining walls.

2

Site Considerations

Determining Grade

To determine existing grades or set new ones, use this formula:
D = G x L

D is the vertical drop in feet; G equals the existing or desired grade as a decimal (2 percent would be 0.02); L equals the horizontal distance in feet.

For example, say you want to slope a 25-foot-long patio a 1 percent grade, the equation would read 0.01 x 25 = 0.25 feet (or 3 inches). This means the low end of your patio should be 3 inches below the high end. For existing or desired grades use G = D/L; for lengths use L = D/G

Creating a Comfortable Climate for Your Patio

A properly designed site can literally extend the comfortable temperature ranges experienced outdoors by several weeks or more. That means a more comfortable patio and backyard beginning earlier in the spring and lasting later into the fall.

MAKING A SITE COOLER OR WARMER

Deciduous trees planted to the south and west of your patio will block the high summer and afternoon sun. Man-made structures that block the sun include overhead pergolas covered with deciduous vines and strategically placed screen walls.

For cold weather, think of ways to admit direct sunlight while blocking cold winds. For example, a patio that is open to the south but bordered by screens of dense vegetation or solid walls in the other directions will be more comfortable than other parts of the yard. This reflected heat can be as much as 10 degrees warmer than outside these spaces.

Breezes. Strategies for admitting cooling winds in the summer include locating your patio so it is directly in the path of the summer wind. Locate walls and vegetation so that summer winds are directed and channeled into the patio. (See "Controlling Breezes," opposite.) A deciduous tree or overhead pergola that shades your patio will also prevent sunlight from directly entering the house. That same wall can act as a buffer against cold winter winds.

Location, Location, Location. If you live in the temperate or cooler regions of the country, the most important overall strategy for locating your patio is to place it to the south, southeast, or southwest side of your house. Here it will receive sun for most of the day, absorb the warming rays, and continue to radiate them back well into the evening. In southern climates, locate your patio to the east or northeast side(s) of the house so that the sun will warm it early in the day when temperatures are relatively cool. In the late afternoon when it's overly warm, a patio located on the east side of a house will be shady. If you live on sloping or

Above You will find it helpful to locate walks along the natural travel routes in your yard.

Opposite Position patios to take the best advantage of your local climate. Plant trees to provide shade.

CONTROLLING BREEZES

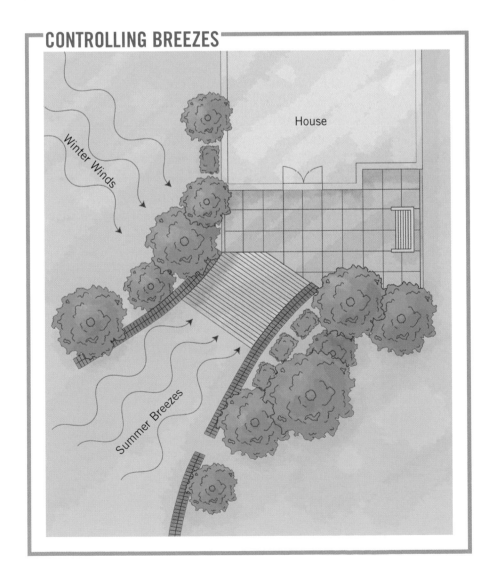

uneven terrain, place your patio on high ground because cold, heavy air collects, much like water, and runs down slopes and into valleys and low spots. A patio located in one of these pockets, called a frost pocket, will be much cooler throughout the year.

Walks

Walks connect or link the areas of your site and make them accessible and useful. Beyond solving just the functional aspects of moving around, you can also design walks so that they are pleasant and provide a sense of enjoyment and delight. There are two approaches you can take when placing walks: you can locate certain areas of your site first and then connect them with your walks, or you can lay out your walks first and then locate the other areas.

Staying on the Right Path. Given the chance, people will generally take the shortest, most direct walk from where they are to where they want to go. We've all seen these lines etched into lawn areas where people cut corners, so to speak, to take a more direct route to their destination. In fact, some professional site planners deliberately leave the sidewalks out of the initial construction phase and, a year or so later, when the walks have been worn into the turf, go back in and build the walks.

This may not be a practical approach for you, but it is an argument against laying out strict 90-degree angled walks. Stay flexible and ask yourself where you really think you'll be walking to get from one place to another on your site.

2

Site Considerations

Shape and Size. Simply put, the major walks should be larger and built out of more elaborate or textured materials than the minor walks. As for the shape of your walks, the basic choices are straight, curved, and angled. Straight walks convey a formal sense to your site. They can also be a little rigid. Curved walks tend to convey an informal or organic feeling to your site.

Curved walks are inherently more flexible and adapt better to sites with slopes and other unusual topography. Don't be afraid to mix different shapes if you feel that's appropriate to your site and needs.

Topography. Topography gets back to one of the main design strategies: always work with the site and not against it. In terms of locating walks, this means avoiding both the steepest areas, which are generally unsafe for most walks, and the lowest spots on your site, where water will collect and damage your walks. On some sites, avoiding slopes and wet spots may be hard. But building through them will also increase your overall costs. The lowest spots on your site may require additional drainage structures, additional fill dirt or gravel to raise the walk above the surrounding grade, or extensive maintenance to keep those portions safe and usable throughout the year.

Safety. Above all, walks must be safe. Features that add to the safety of walks include textured surfaces to improve traction, lighting at critical points such as steps and landings, and sloped "washes" so that water does not collect or remain on the walkway surface itself. To creatre a textured surface, use a common straw broom to add a light, medium, or heavy texture to a concrete surface after it has been troweled smooth and just before it finishes setting up. Low-level lighting (5 to 25 footcandles) at critical points (steps, landings, changes in direction, and entries) makes these places safer at night and they improve the overall look as well. Easily installed walkway lighting fixtures are readily available at home-improvement stores and can take the form of small ground fixtures, pole-mounted fixtures, or wall-mounted fixtures. Washes are slight tilts of the walk itself to one side or the other so that water will drain off instead of forming puddles.

Above *It is easier for a curved walk to blend in with the site than it is for a straight walk. Curved walks tend to be more organic.*

smart tip

MAINTAIN PRIVACY
When laying out walks, locate them so that the privacy of bedrooms and bathrooms is not compromised.

Tree and Plant Guidelines

Trees and other plants will complement your walk, wall, or patio. Here are a few simple tricks that land-scapers and landscape architects use to help them design plantings for a yard. These same tricks can help you.

- Try to group trees and shrubs into twos and threes. Single plantings appear unnatural and sparse.

- Limit the overall variety of plants around your site so that there is a sense of unity and order versus randomness and chaos.

- Use ground covers and grasses as the floors of the site. Bushes, hedges, and shrubs are the outdoor walls. Tree trunks are the columns when defining outdoor spaces, and tree canopies are the outdoor equivalent of ceilings. With these visual images in mind, your task of designing outdoor spaces becomes much easier.

- Trees and plantings, although obviously natural and organic, can be used in geometric or formal arrangements as well. A well-balanced variety of formal and informal planting arrangements can provide a pleasing contrast and enhance the mood you are looking for.

- Be careful not to plant deep-rooted trees next to your house or directly over underground utility lines.

- Use trees to define and frame your best views and screen or block the undesirable ones.

Above *Walks come in a variety of styles, from formal mortared walks to paving stones set on the ground.*

Below *Design walks—and walls and patios for that matter—that look as though they have always been there.*

Accessibility. Accessiblity goes hand in hand with safety. Any walkway that rises or drops more than 6 inches per 10 feet of horizontal run or length is considered a ramp. In northern climates, ramps can be extremely dangerous when they are covered in snow or ice. If you are designing to meet current Americans with Disabilities Act (ADA) standards, for wheel-chair- or walker-dependent users, the maximum rise permitted for every 12 feet of horizontal run is 1 foot. In addition, current ADA standards require that for every 30 feet of horizontal run or length, a level landing of at least 5 feet must be provided for resting. Also, handrails must be provided on both sides of the ramp no matter how high it is.

Designing Your Site

It's time to put pencil to paper, and design the walk, wall, or patio that's right for your yard. The key to it all is a simple scale drawing of your yard that takes into account the terrain, the house, and the neighborhood.

Take a look at your yard. What size is it? Where is the house? The building department is going to ask you the same questions, and the easiest and most precise answer is a simple map. If you know where the property corners are, you can draw your own. If not, look at the plat map, found at your title company or county tax assessor's office. (A quick search through your house purchase records might also produce a small copy of the plat map.) Depending on the age of your house, you might also be able to obtain a site plan with these dimensions from the builder or from the building department, which typically requires a dimensioned site plan before issuing a building permit. Once you've verified the size and shape of the house and lot, take an inventory of a few other important things.

Utility Easements and Street Rights of Way. You may own it, but you don't want to build on part of the land that's been given to a utility company as an easement. A quick call to your local utility companies can tell you if there are any utility easements running through or alongside your property. Sometimes this information can be found on your title insurance report as well. Depending on your situation, you might also want to check with the local transportation department about the street and alley right-of-way. Often, there are restrictions on what can be constructed within a right of way. Street widening projects could have an adverse affect on your plans.

Utility Lines. While you're talking to the utility companies, find out where the sewer,

Left To be on the safe side, be sure to review your plans with the local building department.

Right Some communities have regulations that govern height of fences and walls.

gas, water, power, cable TV, and telephone lines are. All utility companies have maps that show the approximate location of their underground utilities. This is accurate enough for your site plan. Before you begin actual construction, though, call and have these companies locate their lines and the depths exactly. This service is normally free to all utility customers, and many utility districts have a single toll-free number to call for this service. Check the front of your phone book. Once notified and given the address, utility companies will come to your house and mark the site (usually with different colors of spray paint) to show exactly where and how deep their respective lines are located. Take advantage of this free service. Water and sewer utilities are normally buried quite deep to avoid frost and freezing. Other utilities, however, are often in rather shallow trenches and can easily be cut when digging trenches for a walk or wall.

Zoning. City and county zoning ordinances usually have no affect on site-related improvements. Walks, walls, and patios are normally excluded from front-, side-, and rear-yard setbacks. Only enclosed buildings such as houses, garages, and sheds are required to stay behind these setback lines. On the other hand, it pays to visit the local planning department and verify just how your property is zoned and what effect that could have on your plans.

Legal Restrictions. Most newer subdivisions will have a set of covenants, codes, and restrictions (CCRs) that can affect the type of materials used and perhaps some other aspects of your project. Your property deed or your title insurance report should have this information.

Become familiar with these requirements before designing: this will help you avoid any unpleasant surprises down the road. If you live in an older neighborhood, check with the local planning department to see if any historic district restrictions apply to your site.

Natural Physical Features. Note and record existing trees and vegetation you'll want to save. Be on the lookout for rock outcrops, shallow layers of bedrock, or extremely rocky soils you'll want to avoid. Note drainage swales, ditches, ponds, or streams and the soil type(s) on your site. Perhaps the most important natural feature to observe and record is the topography of your site. This means accurately measuring and locating all the sloping areas, flat areas, high points, ridges, mounds, low points, and valleys. This is important for two reasons: first, it tells you what the drainage patterns are. Second, it provides a basis for working with your site contours during the design process instead of against them.

Man-made Features. Along with the natural features of your site, record any man-made improvements, such as existing fences, walks, retaining walls, curb cuts, utility poles, fire hydrants, and any other elements or details that will impact your landscaping plans. Measure and record these items in relation to a fixed reference point, such as the corner of your house, shed, or garage.

Climate Conditions. Unless you live in a one-season climate, check with your local weather bureau, airport, or university to find information on your particular climate. Things to look for include average monthly amounts of rainfall and snowfall, average monthly temperatures, typical wind directions for both summer and winter months, and the seasonal sun angles for your location. This type of information is easy to obtain and can be extremely helpful when you get ready to locate features such as patios or planting beds.

Views and Vistas. No site inventory would be complete without noting the best, and worst, views from the site. Good views are a special site amenity that should be preserved and, if possible, enhanced through careful planning and design. Technically, a view is an open sweep of landscape such as distant mountains or the seaside, while a vista is a portion of that view, usually with a single element as its focus. As you design your new site plan, make the most of your best views by opening them up from important locations on your site. Conversely, use this chance to screen or block unwanted, undesirable views.

Making a Site Plan

Now that you've spent some time inventorying your yard and thinking about what you want to include on your site, it's time to organize your thoughts by drawing up a site plan. There's a logical sequence to preparing site plans and drawings. In general terms, the drawings proceed from the large elements of the plan and progress toward the smallest elements and details.

The first step is to make a rough sketch of your site, including the house and the shape of the yard. Begin with the existing deed map, site plan, or plat map you gathered earlier. Reproduce it exactly on a large piece of tracing paper with graph lines on it (available at stationery

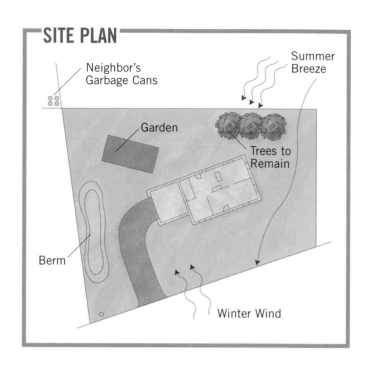

SITE PLAN

Neighbor's Garbage Cans

Summer Breeze

Garden

Trees to Remain

Berm

Winter Wind

shops or art supply stores). For large landscape projects, draw the entire property: show its overall dimensions, its orientation (relative to north), the location of the house and other buildings, and setback distances and easements from property lines, buildings, and street(s). For smaller projects, just draw the affected portion of the property.

The base map should also show your house's floor plan. If you have architect's blueprints of your house, use them to show the location of exterior doors, as well as windows for views. Show the location of other buildings and permanent structures on the property, such as existing walks, walls, fences, detached garages, storage sheds, decks, patios, and the like. Show the location of underground utility lines, pipes, and cables. Draw in the size and location of existing plantings, such as trees, hedges, and shrubs as well as lawn areas, planting beds, and borders. Indicate which trees and shrubs are to be kept and which will need to be removed or relocated during the project.

Rough Layout. Now the fun begins. Attach an overlay of tracing paper to the base map. This is where you should begin sketching and actually placing your outdoor areas. Begin with very loose diagrams as you try out different locations

ROUGH LAYOUT

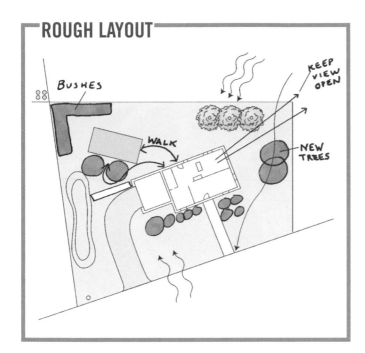

FINAL LAYOUT

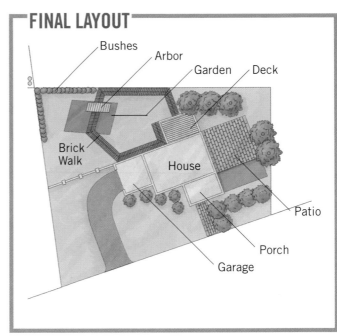

for the walks, walls, and patio(s) on your site. The quicker and looser these early sketches are, the better. This allows you to try out many different ideas, locations, and configurations rapidly and without having to commit to the very first plan layout or idea that you have.

Final Layout. Don't like what you've done? Tear off the overlay and start over. Want to improve on a pretty good design? Add another overlay, and edit your design as you trace it. Keep drawing and improving until you're happy with what you see. Then take a little time to reflect on the design itself. Ask someone familiar with your site to review your design. Oftentimes, designers get so close to and wrapped up in their designs that it is literally hard to see the forest for the trees.

Make sure the design fulfills your intended purpose. If you plan to do a lot of entertaining on your patio, make sure it is large enough to comfortably accommodate the number of guests that you expect will visit at one time. Ask yourself if the design fits the site, the house, and the surrounding neighborhood. Make sure the design creates a memorable experience for friends and family. Does it have physical or sensory elements that would make the typical visitor want to return? Have you combined walks,

walls, and patios in such a way as to create a pleasing atmosphere or mood that will be remembered? Make sure you can build your design on your budget. We all want the moon, but take a hard look at the estimated costs for what you intend to build.

Make sure your design minimizes maintenance requirements, such as cleaning, sweeping, mowing, watering, snow removal, painting, or sealing. Some designs look fantastic on paper and then turn out to be real maintenance headaches.

Once you've answered these questions, you may go back and make some final revisions. But when you're happy with what you see, you're ready to start building. Take a copy of the final site plan with you when you go to obtain the building permit.

smart tip

DESIGN FOR EVERYONE

If someone in your family or among your friends has a disability, review your plans—especially walkways—in light of this fact. How easy will it be for him or her to get around? Will your friend be able to get to all parts of your site or only certain areas? Are the walks wide enough to accommodate someone in a wheelchair? Could your design accommodate ramps in the future if necessary?

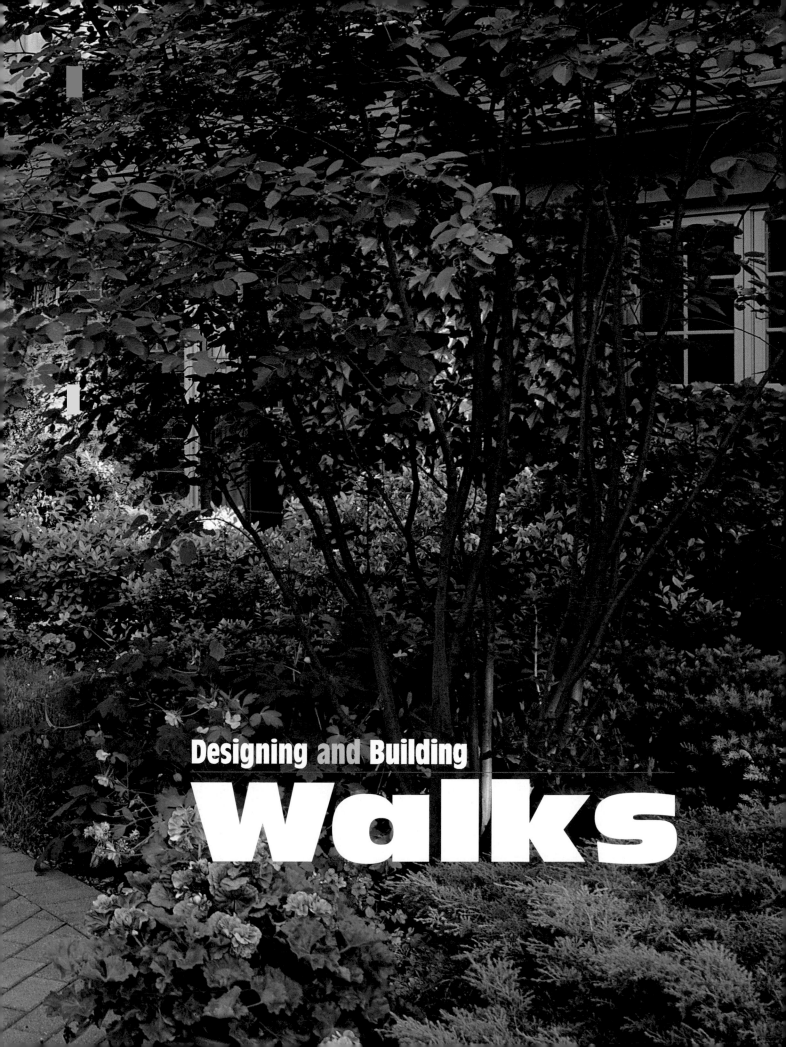

Designing and Building
Walks

Gallery of Walk Designs

1 Two techniques relieve the monotony of this straight walkway: the sculpture area creates a stopping-off spot in the middle of the path, and the brick pattern provides an unusual design touch.

2 This walkway plays a supporting role in this garden. Note how the foliage spills over the edges of the path.

3 Not quite a patio, the bulge within this walkway creates a good spot for a gar den furniture. This design shows how altering walk widths adds to the design interest.

4 Although a short walk, the funnel-like design at its end seems to gather in traffic from the gar den to the porch.

5 This simple undulating walk follows the con tours of the planting bed—a good example of organic design.

Gallery of Walk Designs

1 A wide, well-designed walk can help enhance the front facade of any home.

2 Some walks are so casual they seem more like an afterthought than an actual struc ture. The flowers in the middle of the walk add to the informality of the area.

3 The rigid design of this gravel path brings order to this lush gar den.

4 Broken tiles set in mortar contribute to a unique walkway design.

5 Gravel, wood chips, even mulch can be used to create distinc tive walkways, espe cially in informal areas such as this garden.

3

4

5

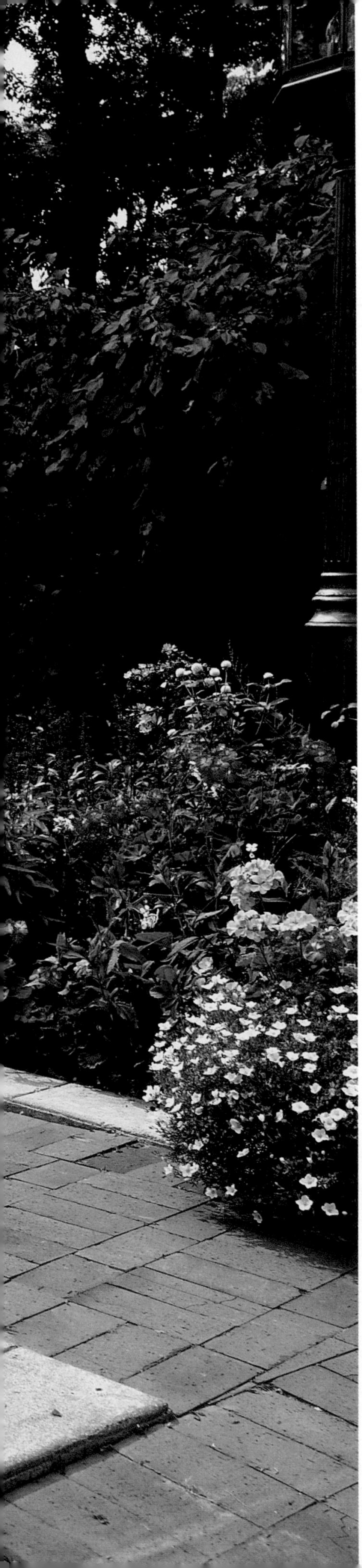

CHAPTER 3

Walk Designs

Hard Walks

Soft Walks

Edging

Grading and Drainage

When you plan a walk, think of it as one part of the overall landscape scheme, complementing fences, gates, walls, patios, decks, planting areas, and other features. These features, along with the characteristics of the site, help you determine the walk's location, design, and materials. This chapter focuses on specific design options and requirements for all kinds of walks.

But you must also think of the walk as something people will use. Even a narrow walk should be a minimum of 2 feet wide, which enables one person to walk comfortably along it. Garden walks that will bear the traffic of wheelbarrows, seed spreaders, and other wheeled equipment should be at least 3 feet wide. Walks 4 feet or wider allow two people to walk comfortably side by side or to pass in opposite directions. Ideally, walks leading to a house's front entry should be 4 feet wide. If you have a wheelchair user in the family, access walks should be at least 5 feet wide.

One of the first decisions you must make when designing a walk is which material to use. Walks can be divided into two basic categories, based on the walk's surface material: hard walks, which are made of brick or stone; and soft walks, which include walks made of wood or loose aggregate.

Hard Walks

Hard walks may be poured concrete or unit masonry materials, such as brick, stone, concrete pavers, and quarry tile. While initial installation can be expensive, hard walks require little maintenance to keep them looking good for many years. Hard walks are preferable in high-traffic areas, such as front entry walks. Choose your materials carefully. A cobblestone or rough flagstone entry walk may look good, but high heels can get caught in the joints. Avoid surfaces that become slippery in the rain, such as glazed ceramic tile. Unglazed quarry tiles are a safer choice.

Most hard walks must be laid on a firm, well-drained subbase or they will tend to buckle, crack, or sink. A subbase consisting of 4 inches of compacted gravel topped by 2 inches of

Left A wide walk constructed of pavers set in concrete provides an air of formality to this entrance.

Right The gazebo serves as a destination at the end of this garden brick paver walk.

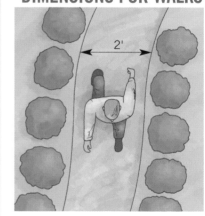

DIMENSIONS FOR WALKS

builder's sand (also called torpedo sand) should suffice. The subbase not only provides a solid, well-drained base but also makes it easier to level the paving units. Poorly drained soils or those subject to frost heave, settling, and erosion may require a subbase of 6 to 8 inches of gravel or crushed stone.

In mild climates, large, relatively flat stones more than 1½ inches thick can also be set directly on level, well-tamped soil or recessed into it. Such walks look quite attractive when the joints between the stones are planted with low-growing ground covers, such as Irish moss, dichondra, or woolly thyme.

The most durable hard walk, however, is a paving material like paving brick, concrete patio blocks, flagstones, or quarry tile laid over a concrete subbase. The concrete—which can be either an existing sidewalk or a new slab—supports the paving material and keeps it from cracking or shifting with freeze-thaw cycles.

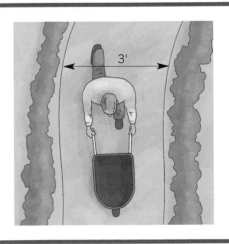

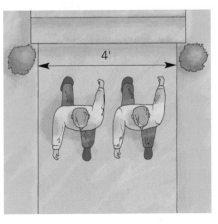

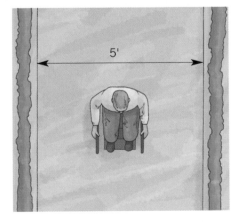

Left A winding gravel walk helps direct traffic in this informal garden setting.

Soft walks usually work best on flat ground—the aggregate can erode if the walk is built on a slope. Also, keep in mind that most loose aggregates make rougher going for wheeled equipment, such as lawn mowers, wheelbarrows, and wheelchairs. Some materials, such as crushed stone and gravel, are tough on bare feet and hard to navigate in dress shoes.

WOOD WALKS

Although naturally decay-resistant woods, such as redwood and cedar, are undeniably beautiful, they are also expensive. Fortunately, the wide availability of treated lumber has made wood practical and economical for walks and edging. Treated wood rated for ground contact may be installed below ground or on grade.

Wood is also a good material for temporary walks: simply attach top boards to flat 2x4 stringers to create modules of any manageable size. You can relocate or rearrange the modules as your landscape requirements change.

Edging

Edging is both decorative and functional. Edging is placed along the sides of a walk to define its borders and to contain the walk material. All soft walks (gravel, bark, and so on) require

Soft Walks

The term soft walks refers to walks that consist of wood or any loose aggregate, such as gravel, decorative rock, crushed shells, wood chips, and bark. Often, these materials are used for walks or paths in rustic or informal garden settings or in areas where only occasional foot traffic is expected. The main advantage of soft walks is that they're relatively easy and inexpensive to install and repair. Unlike masonry walks, soft walks aren't affected by unstable soil or frost heave, so you don't need to be as particular about the base you install beneath them. In fact, the base is often nothing more than tamped dirt.

Loose materials usually have to be replenished annually, however, because the material is kicked into surrounding areas or worked into the soil beneath. To help alleviate these problems, install a sturdy, raised edging to keep the loose paving material from spreading into surrounding areas. It also helps to place landscape fabric on the soil to prevent the paving material from mixing with the earth and to stop weed growth.

EDGING MATERIALS

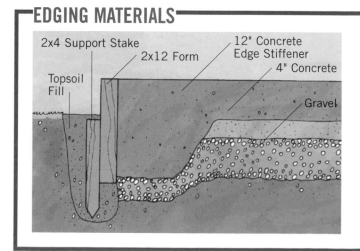

raised edging to keep the material in place. Brick and other masonry walks also need edging if they are to be dry-laid on a sand bed. In such cases, the edging not only holds the pavement in place but also serves to contain the bed on which the paving is set. If the walk materials will be mortared in place, edging is more decorative than structural, and its use is optional. If a concentrated load will be placed at the edge, however, you will need to reinforce the edges. If the walk is located where an automobile will drive over it, for example, you should either pour a thickened concrete edge along each side of the walk or install heavy timbers or railroad ties flush with the concrete surface.

EDGING MATERIALS

Edging materials may be wood, brick, concrete block, stone, or poured concrete, which either can match or contrast with the paving material. Plastic edging, which is completely buried after it's installed, is also available. Wood and plastic edging requires no forms and is simply anchored to the ground with stakes or spikes. When installing most masonry edging, however, you must set up temporary forms to hold the edging units in a straight line and to act as leveling guides.

In choosing edging materials, decide how you want to install them. Most walk surfaces are slightly higher than the surrounding ground. Edging is usually flush with the pavement or slightly recessed to allow for water runoff. If the walk is on or below grade, however, a raised edging keeps surrounding soil from washing onto the walk and serves to contain plantings. A continuous edging of wood or poured concrete can prevent grass and weeds from spreading from the lawn to the walk.

Wood Edging. Pressure-treated landscape ties (usually 4x6s or 6x6s) make massive and sturdy edging that is easy to cut and install. They work with all types of paving materials and can serve as forms for poured-concrete walks—simply leave the timbers in place after the concrete is poured. Plan the excavation so that the edging timbers rest on a 4-inch base of gravel or sand and anchor them in place with rebar spikes.

Below Landscape tie raised above the walk helps contain the soil needed for the planting area.

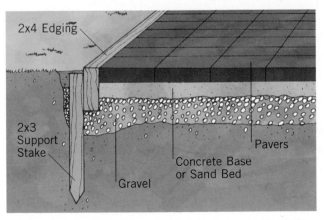

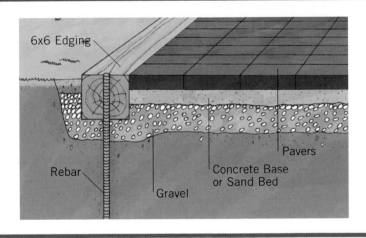

Left *Brick pavers set on end paired with full-face bricks are a classic walkway combination.*

Below *This simple edge treatment almost blends in with the plants, allowing the walk material to take center stage.*

If landscape ties are too massive for your walk design, you can use pressure-treated 2x6s or 2x8s. Set these boards in the ground at the desired height and hold them in place with pressure-treated 2x3 stakes. When the walk is complete, backfill over the stakes with topsoil.

Brick Edging. Bricks make attractive edging that is simple to install in a variety of patterns. It's a good choice for edging curved walks as well. Depending on soil conditions, bricks can be set directly in the ground, or they can be set over a gravel-and-sand sub-base. For more stability, you can set the bricks into a poured-concrete footing.

Block Edging. Concrete edging blocks, manufactured to match patio blocks, may be set in a ribbon of concrete along the walk perimeter. Edging blocks come in straight or curved shapes, with various top designs. The blocks typically measure 24 inches long, 5 inches wide, and 2 inches thick. The edging also may be used by itself as planting borders or in combination with other walk materials.

Stone Edging. Cut stone, cobblestones, and small boulders make good edging for wide walkways. Cut stones, thick flagstones, and cobblestones should be set in a ribbon of concrete to keep them from shifting. Large, irregular boulders can be set in concrete or directly in the ground. For informal walks, you can simply dig a small hole for each stone and place it in the ground. This design will not work in more formal areas. When edging narrow walks, however, you should avoid irregularly shaped stones because they are easily tripped over or kicked out of place. If you're installing a flagstone walk, ask your dealer about the availability of thicker border stones of the same type of rock as you are using on the path.

Concrete Edging. Another alternative to edging brick and other masonry-unit walks is to pour a concrete curb. The curb will require formwork, which can be either straight or curved. A curb 6 to 8 inches wide set 6 to 8 inches in the ground should be adequate for most applications and localities. Place the concrete on a 4-inch bed of gravel or gravel and sand. Before removing the forms, round over the top edges of the concrete with an edging tool.

smart tip

PLASTIC EDGE RESTRAINTS

If you're installing a brick or paver walk and you do not want a visible edging, you can use special molded-plastic edge restraints. Several types are available that will conform to straight or curved walks. To install them, you place the plastic strips along layout lines on the gravel subbase. The edging is held in place with 12-inch spikes driven into the ground. The tops of the plastic edging are used to guide a notched screed board that smoothes the bedding sand. After setting the paving units, you backfill on either side of the walk with topsoil, completely covering the edging, then lay sod or sow seed.

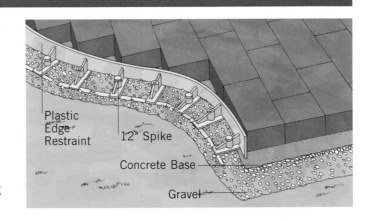

Plastic Edge Restraint

12" Spike

Concrete Base

Gravel

STONE EDGING

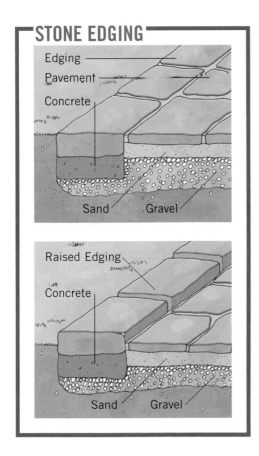

Edging

Pavement

Concrete

Sand   Gravel

Raised Edging

Concrete

Sand   Gravel

Above *Stone pavers of a different color define the borders and make a nice contrast to the red of the brick walkway.*

Grading and Drainage

The characteristics of the site—terrain, soil conditions, and drainage requirements—as well as the paving materials used determine how you must prepare the ground for the walk. Virtually every walk project will require some amount of excavation to create a level surface and to provide a stable base for the paving materials. Installing a walk on a sloped or uneven lot will require extensive cutting and filling to provide a level walking surface. Where the walk runs parallel to a slope, you may need to install low retaining walls on both sides of the walk, as shown below, so that it will be level across its width. If your walk requires extensive grading and excavation, it's best to hire an excavation contractor to do the work.

DRAINAGE

Drainage is usually not a major concern when building a walk. Typically, a building lot is graded so that water runs away from the house, and a walk that runs along grade level presents no problems. In some cases, however, the walk area will have to be graded to provide a slight slope for drainage. If you anticipate drainage problems, sloping the walk ¼ inch per foot along its length will provide adequate drainage in most situations.

In wet soil, you may want to install a perforated drainage pipe in a gravel subbase to assist drainage. If the walk crosses a low area subject to puddling or periodic flooding during the rainy season, loose aggregates, such as gravel or bark, will soon wash away or become mixed with dirt and debris washed in from surrounding areas. In such cases, you should install raised edging and build up the walk materials above the level of the surrounding soil. Don't install walks that cross swales or run across slopes. Such walks can act as dams that impede natural drainage patterns in the yard.

Often, walks made of bricks or concrete pavers are higher in the middle, or crowned, to prevent puddles from gathering on the walk. The crown (measured from the center of the walk to the edge) should

GRADING STEEP SLOPES

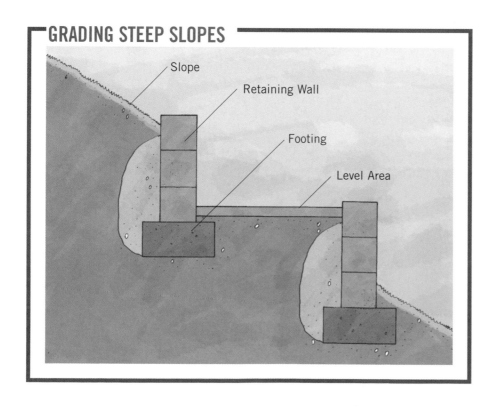

Slope

Retaining Wall

Footing

Level Area

Left Handle a steep slope by creating a series of steps. Here large slate slabs serve as steps.

Right Design hard-material walkways with crowns in the center to help rain and snow to drain off of the path.

be about ⅛ inch per foot. A 4-foot-wide walk, for example, is crowned ¼ inch in the middle. Poured-concrete and flagstone walks are often sloped across their width (about ⅛ inch per foot) to shed water. If a hard walk is next to a garden wall or the house, slope it away from the structure, as shown below right.

CHANGES IN WALK LEVEL

On lots with only minor changes in grade or terrain, a hard-surface walk may be able to follow the contour of the land, provided that the walk doesn't become submerged during the rainy season. But for soft walks, the ground must be level, or the aggregate could wash away from high spots and collect in low spots, leaving bare areas. Steeper slopes or grades are usually dealt with by means of steps. If the slope is fairly gentle, you can install long sections of level walkways interspersed with steps. For steeper slopes, flights of stairs connected by

landings may be the best solution.

To determine how many steps are needed, calculate the total amount of rise between the uphill side of the walk and the downhill side, then divide this measurement by the riser height of each step. (Risers should be no more than 8 inches high.)

DRAINAGE BASICS

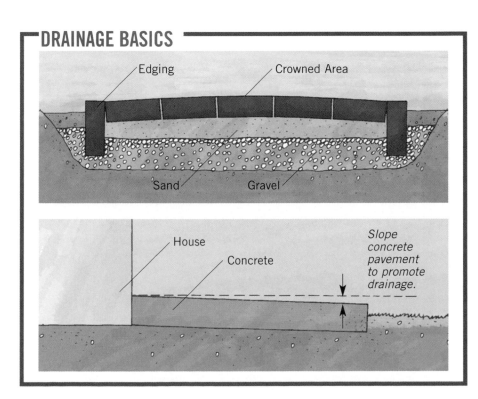

Edging   Crowned Area

Sand   Gravel

House

Concrete

Slope concrete pavement to promote drainage.

Soft Walks

Layout and Preparation

S oft walks are made of loose stones, wood, or wood products. They are less expensive and easier to install than hard walks but will require more maintenance. Because of the variety of materials, they can take on a variety of appearances. Gravel or pebbles come in an array of colors and sizes. Wood walks can be built from boards or from loose aggregate, including bark, wood chips, and mulch.

In most cases, wood walks made from boards require a gravel subbase, but stone and wood loose aggregates may be placed directly on the ground. Usually, edging will be required to contain loose aggregate. Even with edging, however, foot traffic will disperse loose aggregate into the surrounding area, and if the area is a lawn, a lawn-mower blade can turn the aggregate into dangerous projectiles. On the other hand, both stone and wood aggregates will conform to any shape walk, which makes these materials highly desirable for surfacing meandering garden paths.

Lumber walks can take many shapes and can be raised above grade level to bridge rough terrain or low areas. For high-traffic areas, a lumber walk offers the advantages of easy installation and repair and can serve to unify other wood elements, such as a deck or house siding, with the landscape.

Stone

In general, stone aggregate is a good choice for walks that receive light traffic. Because it dries quickly and drains efficiently, crushed stone is a good choice for garden paths. A light spray from a garden hose is usually enough to wash away surface dirt. To cover 100 square feet of walkway with a 2-inch layer of stone, you will need about ⅔ cubic yard of material.

As for its disadvantages, stone must be replenished, raked, and tamped periodically. When compared with a hard walk surface, pushing a wheelbarrow over loose stone requires more effort, and walking in dress shoes or barefoot can be difficult, if not painful.

TYPES OF STONE AGGREGATE

Stones used for soft walks may be classified by their texture, either smooth or rough. Generally, rough stones make a tighter, more compact walk than do smooth stones. Both textures are available in many colors and sizes, but choose carefully. Pick a color that won't overwhelm the landscape—blue rocks that look attractive in the bag may end up as an electric blue river in your yard. Also consider function. Light-colored stones stain easily, so they won't be appro-

Left Loose gravel or other aggregate materials make great informal walks. They are attractive and easy to build. But gravel and similar materials often require periodic replenishing.

priate for a high-traffic path, like one the rototiller takes to the garden.

Although loose aggregate ranges from ¼-inch pebbles to 3-inch stones, the best sizes are between ¾ and 1½ inches. This is a good size to choose because these medium-size stones stay in place better than small pebbles, and they compact better and are more comfortable to walk on than large stones.

Gravel and Crushed Stone. You can buy gravel or crushed stone in uniform sizes or in random sizes, called unscreened gravel. Because gravel is jagged, it compacts well, but it's also uncomfortable to walk on barefoot. Typically blue-gray in color, gravel is also commonly available as reddish-brown redrock, white dolomite, and multicolored decomposed granite.

Smooth Aggregates. River stone is smooth, which makes it more comfortable to walk on barefoot but less likely to stay compacted. River stone usually consists of white, tan, and gray rocks, which have been rounded smooth either naturally or by machine. Like gravel, river stone is sold in a variety of sizes by the bag or by the yard at stone yards and garden centers.

BASES FOR SOFT WALKS

Loose Aggregate Walk

Gravel, Bark, or Other Fill   Brick Edging

Landscape Fabric   Tamped Soil

Boardwalk

2x4 Sleeper   2x6 Deck Board

Landscape Fabric   Tamped Gravel

Wood

Loose wood-aggregate walks are simpler and less expensive to install than lumber walks, but they won't last nearly as long. Bark, wood chips, and mulch make a soft, springy walkway that you can kneel on comfortably when gardening. Like stone, wood aggregates are recommended for light-traffic areas and are diffi-

Plotting Curves

Curved walks can be laid out in a freeform design or by "drawing" a series of arcs on the ground with a giant compass, made from a rope, a stake, and a sharp stick. Tie one end of the rope to the stake and drive it into the ground. Mark the desired radius on the rope, and tie the stick at the mark. Swing the rope and stick around the stake, scratching the arc on the ground. Adjust the length of the rope to lay out the other side of the walk.

Lay out an irregular curve with a rope or garden hose. Outline one side of the curve with the rope or hose. Cut a series of sticks the width of the walk, and place them at regular intervals, as shown. Outline the other side of the curve with a second rope or hose. Then sprinkle flour or sand to mark the curves. Dig a trench deep enough to accommodate a curved form (which can be made from bending thin plywood) or a permanent edging material, such as bricks.

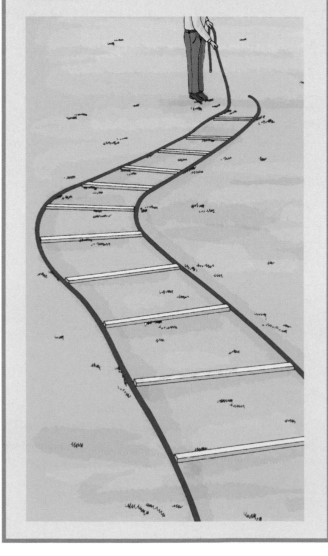

cult to negotiate with wheeled equipment or in high heels. Most wood aggregates will last only a few years before decomposing. Bark and redwood chips will last longer but are expensive. Wood aggregates tend to hold moisture, and they will wash away in a heavy rain, leaving bare spots. Avoid them in areas subject to flooding or with poor drainage. Even under good circumstances, the wood aggregates require regular raking and replenishing. To cover 100 square feet of walkway with a 2-inch layer of wood aggregate, you will initially need about ⅔ cubic yard of the material.

Bark Chips. Sold by the bag, bark chips come in a variety of sizes, from ¼ to 3 inches. Two common types, firbark and tanbark, have a dark color and a rustic texture that complement a natural landscape. Generally, bark lasts longer but is more expensive than wood chips.

Wood Chips. Typically light in color, wood chips are the by-product of milling or tree-clearing operations. Wood chips sold by the bag are purer than those sold by the yard, which often contain leaves, twigs, and bark, but the bagged form is also more expensive. Landscapers and utility companies sometimes sell wood chips at reasonable prices by the truckload.

Mulch. Mulch refers to a variety of organic materials cut to small sizes, such as ground bark, sawdust, conifer needles, and shredded roots. Among all loose aggregates, mulch offers the most comfortable walking surface.

Loose-Aggregate Walk

In circumstances where drainage is not a problem, soft walk materials can be placed in a shallow excavation, with edging installed in trenches on each side of the walk. It's not necessary to build up a gravel subbase. Simply tamp the soil at the bottom of the excavation.

Excavate the site. Begin by laying out the walk with stakes and string. First, drive two 1x2

Loose-Aggregate Walk

TOOLS

- Spade (for removing sod)
- Rake or hoe
- Hand or mechanical tamper
- Rubber mallet
- Stakes and string

MATERIALS

- Landscape fabric
- Gravel
- Bricks for edging

1 *Dig narrow trenches* on each side of the walkway to hold the brick edging.

2 *Spread landscape sheeting* to stop weed growth. Place bricks in trench and backfill with soil.

3 *Bed bricks* by tapping with a mallet (inset). Add aggregate and tamp with hand or power tamper.

stakes at each end of the walk, positioned to indicate the edges of the walk. Then attach string to the stakes to mark the finished height of the edging—usually about 2 inches above grade. Don't level the string; if the ground slopes, the string should slope with it. Check to make sure that the string is the same distance apart at both ends.

Dig the Edging Trenches. Use a flat-bladed shovel to dig narrow trenches for the edging. **1** Dig the trenches deep enough so that the edging just touches the top of the string. Lay down landscape fabric to discourage weed growth, tucking the fabric into the edging trenches.

Install the Edging. Double-check to make sure the strings are at the right height, and use them as a guide in installing straight edging. As you set brick and block edging, fill behind them with compacted soil. **2**

Spread the Loose Aggregate. Add the soft walk material in 1-inch layers, spreading and tamping each layer until the material is within ¾ inch of the top of the edging. **3** The walk sur-

Subsurface Drainage

If you are building a walk in an area that is subject to flooding, such as a walk at the bottom of a slope, you'll dig the walk an extra 6 inches deep and lay a 4-inch perforated drainpipe down the middle. Dig the middle of the excavation a few inches deeper than along the sides to create a sloping bottom that aids in drainage.

Spread and tamp a 2-inch layer of gravel (crushed limestone works best) on the bottom. Set the perforated pipe in the middle of the excavation with the perforations down. Continue filling until you can set edging on the fill and have it protrude about 2 inches above grade. If you are setting brick edging, lean the bricks against the sides of the excavation. If the soil will not hold a vertical edge, prop the bricks against wood forms. Add stone to cover the pipe, but leave enough room for a 2-inch layer of walk material. Place a layer of landscape fabric on the crushed gravel, then spread the surface material until it comes within about ¾ inch of the top of the edging.

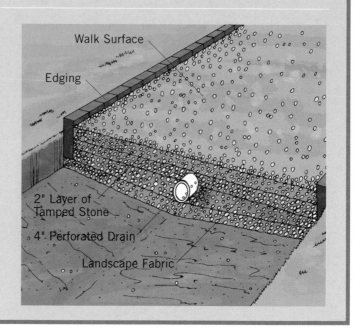

face should be above the surrounding grade. Bed brick or block edging by tapping the inside face of the edging with a rubber mallet.

Lumber Walks

Compared with most hard walk materials, such as concrete and brick, lumber is easy to cut and install. It's less expensive than most paving materials, and depending on the type of lumber you choose, a wood walk may last as long as a hard walk. To build a lumber walk, all you need are a few basic layout and carpentry tools, a shovel, a rake, and a wheelbarrow. If you're laying the walk on or below grade, you should provide a level, well-drained base of gravel.

Some lumber species, notably redwood, cypress, and cedar, are naturally resistant to decay and can be used to construct wood walks, albeit expensive ones. A more economical approach is to use pressure-treated lumber. You can install a durable, long-lasting treated-wood walk in, on, or above the ground. Building an above-ground walk is an excellent way to avoid altering existing

drainage patterns or to create a level walking surface across uneven or rocky terrain with a minimum of excavation.

TREATED LUMBER

Treated wood comes in a variety of dimensional sizes, from one-by boards to large landscape timbers and poles. All treated wood is rated according to usage. Lumber rated for ground contact, designated 0.41 (meaning it has a preservative retention of 0.41 pound per cubic foot), is recommended for all walk applications. Preservative doesn't completely penetrate into the center of the board, so you should apply wood preservative to the cut ends. If your design calls for large timbers, use treated landscape ties. Treated timbers are better for walking on than real railroad ties, which are splintery and have a toxic, oily creosote coating

UNTREATED LUMBER

Naturally decay-resistant woods, such as redwood and cedar, are often used in outdoor projects for appearance's sake. Such woods are recommended for aboveground use only, where they may last 10 years or more, depending on climate and maintenance. Finishing such wood species with paint, stain, or preservative will prolong the life span. Other species, such as pine and fir, have little resistance to decay and are not recommended for walks even if finished.

Wood Rounds and Blocks. In some part of North America (typically in the West), redwood and cedar rounds are used as "stepping stones." Rounds are sections of log about 3 to 6 inches thick and 12 to 30 inches in diameter, with or without the bark attached. Laid directly on level, well-drained soil or on a compacted-sand base, the rounds last about five years before they begin to decay. (Simulated wood rounds, which are formed from concrete, are available at stone yards and patio suppliers and will last much longer.) Plant the spaces between rounds with a ground cover that can withstand light foot traffic. Such plants include Irish moss, lippia, sandwort, and yerba linda. You can also recess the rounds into a soft walk made from a loose aggregate, such as gravel or bark chips. The rounds should be about ½ inch higher than the surrounding loose aggregate so that it won't wash over the rounds.

If wood rounds aren't available in your area, but you like exposed end-grain, you can set short timber blocks (either redwood or pressure-treated lumber) vertically in a sand bed. The procedure is similar to that for setting bricks in sand. (See "Laying Paving Units in Sand," page

90.) Cut the blocks—4x6s or larger timbers—into 3- or 4-inch lengths. Lay enough blocks to calculate the width of the walk. Excavate the walk area; add a gravel-and-sand base; and install the edging before setting the blocks. To avoid drainage problems, set the edging so it will be flush with, or below, the walk surface. Put the blocks end-grain up, and butt them together. Sweep fine sand into the joints.

After setting rounds or timber blocks, brush on a good water sealer or a wood preservative to help prevent checking and cracking. Soaking the blocks or rounds in a wood preservative before installation will extend their life considerably, although the treatment is fairly expensive. Because many wood preservatives are toxic, follow all label precautions

Boardwalks

You can build a simple wooden boardwalk by nailing two-by crosspieces to wood sleepers laid either in or on top of a flat, well-drained base of gravel. Make the sleepers from treated wood rated for ground contact. The deck boards can be treated wood or a decay-resistant species. Support walks more than 3 feet wide with a third sleeper running down the center of the walk. For wider walks, space sleepers no more than 3 feet apart.

LUMBER WALK OPTIONS

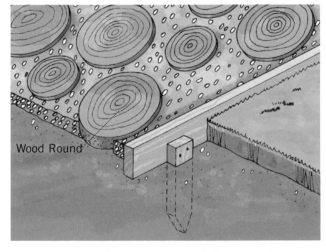

Wood Round

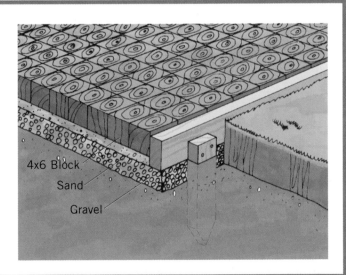

4x6 Block

Sand

Gravel

The walk surface should be at least 1½ inches above grade. To keep washed soil and trash from accumulating underneath the raised walk, attach a two-by header that touches the ground at each end.

The decking can be 2x6s, 2x8s, or wider boards, or a combination of widths. The project described below uses 2x4 sleepers laid flat on top of a gravel subbase. The 3-foot-wide walk surface is 2x6 deck boards.

BUILDING A BOARDWALK

At each end of the walk, drive two 1x2 stakes at least 2 feet into the ground to indicate the edges of the walk, and stretch strings between them. Double-check to make sure that the strings are the same distance apart at both ends. If the walk leads straight to an entry, make sure the lines are perpendicular to it by using the 3-4-5 triangulation method, explained in "Using the 3-4-5 Method," page 153.

Build the Base. If you are building on stable, well-drained soil, you can lay the walk directly on the ground. If the ground is soggy or prone to puddles, build a gravel base for the walk. First, dig a trench at least 4 inches deep and wider than the walk by 4 to 6 inches on each side. **1**

To prevent weed growth, lay landscape fabric over the bottom of the excavation. Backfill with 4 inches of pea gravel and tamp, or with 2 inches of pea gravel and 2 inches of sand. Tamp each layer as you install it. **2**

Install the Sleepers. Use the layout strings to position the sleepers on the gravel base. For sleepers that are flush with the ends of the boards, align the sleepers with the layout lines. For overhanging boards, align a 2x4 spacer with the lines and lay the sleeper next to the spacer. **3** In either case, lay the sleepers flat on the ground and drive 2x4 stakes every 4 feet along the inside edges of the sleepers. Attach the sleepers to the stakes by driving 3-inch galvanized deck screws through the stakes. Where sleepers butt together, join them with 1x4 cleats on the inside of the sleepers. Drive stakes on either side of the cleat.

Attach the Decking. Cut 2x6 decking boards to length. Align the boards with a framing square, and attach them to the sleepers with 10d galvanized nails or 3-inch deck screws. **4** Predrill holes to avoid splitting board ends.

If you are using redwood or cedar decking, leave a ⅛- to ¼-inch space between boards to allow for wood expansion, and to facilitate water runoff—16d common nails make good spacers.

To give the walk a finished look, use a router with a round-over bit to give the edges of the walk a smooth, uniform look. **5**

Plank Walks

A variation of the boardwalk is a plank walk. In this type of wood walk, 2x8 or wider deck boards run along the length of the walk and are supported by 2x4 cleats laid across the walk excavation. Letting the deck boards overhang the cleats is not advisable, so cut the cleats to the exact walk width and set them every 3 feet directly on a gravel base. Lay the first plank over the cleats, aligned with the layout line; when the end of a cleat is flush with the edge of the plank, fasten the two together. Make sure joints between planks occur over cleats. Use a framing square to keep the cleats perpendicular to the planks. For a finished appearance (and additional stability), attach 2x4 or 2x6 edge strips around the walk perimeter.

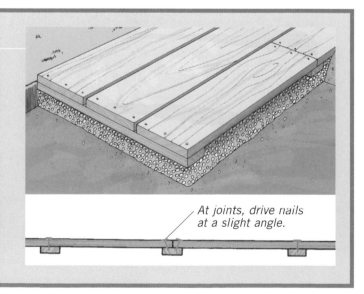

At joints, drive nails at a slight angle.

Building a Boardwalk

TOOLS	MATERIALS
◼ Spade or shovel	◼ Gravel
◼ Rake or hoe	◼ Landscape fabric
◼ Hand or mechanical tamper	◼ Treated lumber for sleepers
◼ Drill Driver	◼ Lumber for walk
◼ Router	
◼ Round-over bit	
◼ Tape Measure	
◼ Stakes and strings	

1 **Dig the trench** at least 4 in. deep and 4 to 6 in. wider than the walk on each side.

2 **Install landscape fabric;** add a 4 in. deep layer of gravel. Rake and tamp as needed.

3 **Install the sleepers.** Use two-by lumber attached to stakes driven into the ground.

4 **Attach the boards** to the sleepers with 3-in.-long decking screws.

5 **Finish the edges** with a router equipped with a round-over bit. This will provide a smooth finish.

Dry-Laid Walks

Flexible Paving. For dry-laid walks, the joints between paving materials are filled with sand, topsoil, or dry mortar. The width of the joints will help you determine which joint-filling material to use. Paving materials that can be laid closely together, such as bricks and interlocking pavers, are usually set with sand between the joints. In this type of construction, called flexible paving, fine mason's sand is swept into the joints, creating a stable and durable walk, even in climates subject to some frost heave. It's easy to replace damaged paving materials, fill sunken portions of the walk, or remove sections of the walk to get to buried utility lines or pipes. However, the sand must be replenished annually, and sometimes more frequently.

Wide Joints. Joints between irregularly shaped paving materials, such as flagstones and rubble, are too wide to hold onto sand, so these paving materials have topsoil or mortar joints. If you live in an area where frost heave is not a problem, you can make a simple and attractive walk by setting concrete stepping stones, flagstones (2 inches or thicker), or fieldstones directly on compacted soil. Pack the joints with topsoil. To prevent weed growth, plant the crevices with grass or a low-growing ground cover. Mortared joints make for a smoother, more formal walk than topsoil joints, but they are subject to cracking in a dry-laid walk.

This chapter and the next concern hard walks, made of unit paving materials—brick, concrete pavers, and stone. There are two ways to set these walks: you can dry-lay them or set them in wet mortar. This chapter discusses dry-laid walks, in which paving materials are laid on a bed of tamped sand over gravel. The next discusses laying paving material in mortar on top of a concrete bed.

Tools You Will Need

The tools you will need for installing a dry-laid walk will depend on the walk material, but some tools will be used for all walks. For example, the job of compacting the soil and subbase can be done with a hand tamper; however, renting a power tamper is recommended. Power tampers compact soil, gravel, and sand better, faster, and with less effort than tamping by hand.

Screed Board. You can make a screed board to smooth the sand bed. The screed board is a section of 1x6, the ends of which are notched to fit loosely inside the walk borders or edgings. Because the notched ends usually ride on top of the edgings, the notch depth equals the thickness of the paving material. If you're laying dimensional paving materials, such as brick or dressed stone, cut the screed board so that the bottom edge is arched the proper amount to create a crowned walk. When setting irregular paving materials, such as flagstones and rubble, the board is straight because the walk is pitched sideways to shed water.

Opposite For paving materials of a consistent size, such as bricks or concrete pavers, use mason's sand to fill the joints.

Right Placing large paving stones directly on compacted soil creates an informal walk.

USING A SCREED BOARD

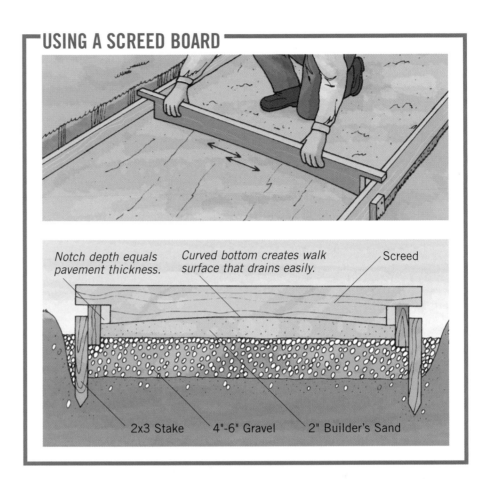

Notch depth equals pavement thickness.

Curved bottom creates walk surface that drains easily.

Screed

2x3 Stake   4"-6" Gravel   2" Builder's Sand

5

Dry-Laid Walks

Material Selections

Paving materials that can be laid in a sand bed over a gravel subbase include brick, stone, adobe, concrete patio blocks, and interlocking pavers. Among these choices, some materials are cut to more precise sizes and shapes than others; some materials are better suited to particular climates. Otherwise, walk construction techniques and required substrates are similar for all of the common paving materials. Exceptions are noted under each heading below. As with any masonry project, check local building codes for specific requirements and accepted practices in your area.

Right Brick pavers are a good material to use when you want to create an undulating walkway.

Below Brick is one of the few materials that looks good in both formal and informal settings.

BRICK

Bricks provide a beautiful walk surface that will last for many years, provided that you choose the right kind of brick. That's a formidable task, considering that bricks come in a bewildering array of sizes, colors, and textures, not all of which are suitable for walks. Some bricks are designed for interior applications and won't hold up under wet or freezing conditions; some have smooth or glazed surfaces that can make for a dangerously slippery walk when wet. The ideal brick is hard and dense and has a slightly rough surface to provide good traction in wet weather. Paving brick is designed especially for walks and patios and meets these criteria. The next best choice is face brick, followed by concrete brick.

Paving Brick. Designed especially for ground contact, paving brick is sealed, so it has a high resistance to abrasion and moisture penetration.

Most paving bricks are cut to uniform dimensions in modular sizes, so they can be set with perfectly aligned, mortarless joints. You can also get pavers that are sized to work with mortar joints. Some paving bricks, called repress pavers, have chamfered or rounded edges on one or both faces. Repress pavers are preferred in some climates because the chamfered edges facilitate water runoff and are less likely to chip if struck by a snow shovel.

Concrete Brick. If you live in a mild climate and your walk will receive only light traffic, you can save money by using concrete brick. Concrete bricks are not quite as durable as pavers, and their colors, sizes, and textures are often limited. A typical concrete brick measures 2¼ x 3⅝ x 7⅝ inches. Because this is a manufactured product, the size and coloring are usually very consistent. Unfortunately, the pigments used to color the concrete sometimes fade. As with concrete blocks and pavers, the bricks have a slightly rough, pitted surface.

Durability. Most clay bricks are manufactured to withstand the weather. The most expensive grade, SX paving bricks, will withstand severe weathering, such as freeze-thaw conditions in cold climates and are recommended for outdoor walks and patios. MX paving bricks will withstand moderate weather conditions, including rain and mild frost. Before you start your project, consult your local building department for information on the brick types that are suitable for your particular area and project. Bricks are also rated for hardness. The hardest, Type I, is the most expensive, but it is rarely used in residential applications. Type II is suitable for residential driveways and entry walks, and Type III is adequate for low-traffic garden walks and patios.

Estimating Bricks. Pavers designed to be used with mortar joints are usually referred to by their nominal size—the actual size plus the width of a mortar joint. Pavers designed for swept-sand joints usually have spacer nubs that leave space for the sand. Whether or not you are using joints, it will take an average of 4.5 bricks to cover a square foot. For example, a 12-foot-by-20-foot patio is 240 square feet. Multiply 240 x 4.5 bricks to find you need 1,080 bricks. Order 5 to 10 percent extra to allow for miscuts, breakage, and future repairs.

Certain brick patterns, such as herringbone and basket weave, require a brick type with a length that is exactly twice its width if the bricks will be set without mortar joints. A standard modular brick works well for these patterns—it has a nominal size of 2⅔ inches thick, 4 inches wide, and 8 inches long.

Split pavers are half the thickness of a standard brick and are useful when headroom is limited, such as in an enclosed porch. Soap bricks are half the width of a standard brick. Soaps are sometimes used as border bricks for walks or to create special patterns within the paving area.

Cutting Bricks. If your walk requires a few cut bricks, you can cut them with a brick chisel, or brickset, and small sledgehammer. To cut a brick with a chisel, first mark the cut line with a piece of chalk or grease pencil. With a hammer and brickset, tap all four sides of the brick to score it along the cut line; then center the brickset over the line and strike the chisel sharply. You may have to strike the brickset a few times.

smart tip

GETTING CLEAN CUTS
A brick splitter produces cleaner and more precise cuts than you can achieve with a hammer and chisel. You can rent them from a tool rental outlet. Another option is a circular saw equipped with a masonry blade.

BRICK PATTERNS

Bricks require careful layout to avoid mis-aligned joints or partial bricks along the edges of the walk. Before you lay the bricks, do a dry run to spot any potential layout problems.

Jack-on-Jack. Also called a stack bond, this pattern is the simplest to lay and the least interesting. Starting at one end of the walk, place a single brick in one corner, then place remaining

bricks in stair-step fashion, in the sequence shown. If possible, plan the walk width to avoid cut bricks. If you can't do this, cut the bricks you'll need to the same size, all at once with a masonry saw. Place cut bricks along the least conspicuous edge of the walk, such as against a building or overhanging plant border.

Running Bond. This is the most popular brick pattern and is easy to lay out. Also, the pattern

POPULAR BRICK PATTERNS

Jack-on-Jack

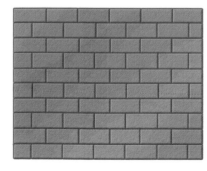

Running Bond

Herringbone

Far left A three-brick basket-weave pattern helps this walk stand out in this overgrown garden.

Center The brick pattern shown here carries the eye from one side of the water feature to the other.

Left The running-bond pattern is a classic choice for straight, formal walks.

bond design, a herringbone pattern requires partial bricks along the walk edges and ends, which are best cut in advance on a masonry saw. Starting at one corner, place full bricks in the step pattern shown, using half bricks to fill in along the edges. Use a framing square to align bricks meeting at right angles.

Weaves. Basket-weave designs look best when you use modular bricks on which the nominal width is exactly half the length. To make a simple two-brick basket weave, lay two bricks side by side to form a square in one corner of the walk. Working across the walk, lay a second square of two bricks at right angles to the first. Alternate the direction of each square until you reach the other side of the walk. Install the second course by laying two bricks at right angles to the square above it. Continue in this manner to create the pattern shown. Start the half-basket weave as shown, beginning the second course with bats, a brick that is cut in half lengthwise.

The ladder weave combines the weave patterns with the Jack-on-Jack pattern.

visually minimizes any minor variations in brick sizes. Place the first course of bricks end to end across the walk. Start the second course with a half brick, followed by whole bricks placed end to end so that joints fall midway between bricks as shown.

Herringbone. This pattern looks best on wide walks. On walks 3 feet wide or less, the pattern may appear confusing. As with the running-

---

Basket Weave

Half-Basket Weave

Ladder Weave

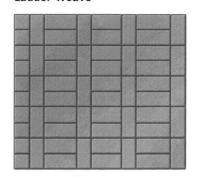

ADOBE BLOCKS

With its earthy tan color characteristic of south-western and early California architecture, adobe lends a warm, natural feel to the garden. Because traditional adobe is not waterproof, it's used mostly in warm, arid climates. Modern adobe paving blocks, however, are nearly as waterproof as clay bricks. Adobe paving blocks come in a variety of square and rectangular sizes.

Consider using small, brick-size units for walks; large blocks may be out of scale in the landscape. Most adobe block is produced in the Southwest and California, where it is inexpensive compared with standard clay brick. Elsewhere, shipping costs make adobe more expensive.

Installation. Lay adobe on a gravel-and-sand bed, as you would brick. (Follow the instructions in "Laying Paving Units in Sand," page 90.) The sand bed should be perfectly smooth and pitched slightly across its width to shed water. Set the bricks with wide (¾- to 1-inch) joints to compensate for the irregularity of the brick edges and to provide sufficient drainage. Pack the joints with sand or well-draining soil. Do not use mortar, which can stain the adobe. Jack-on-Jack and running bond are two popular patterns.

smart tip

POWER TAMPING
For large projects, do your arms and shoulders a favor by renting a vibrating tamper. You can use it to smooth out gravel and to make sure the paving material is set firmly.

STONE

Natural stone walks lend a sense of permanence to the landscape and blend with almost any decor. Stone comes in a variety of colors, shapes, and sizes. The most common types used for walks and patios are split along natural fissure lines to produce a slender, flat stone. Such stones include slate, quartzite, and sandstone. These and many other types of split, or "cleft," stones are available as flagstones and dimensioned paving stones, but you'll usually be limited to what's available in your area.

Ashlar. Ashlar is cut to square or rectangular shapes either in random or uniform sizes to present a more formal appearance. Typically, such stones are laid in a coursed pattern.

Flagstone. Flagstones—usually slate, limestone, or sandstone slabs—come in random shapes and sizes and are fitted together like a jigsaw puzzle in a random pattern. Generally, flagstones are less expensive than ashlar.

Fieldstone. As their name implies, fieldstones are rocks collected from fields, dry creek bottoms, and similar sources. Most fieldstones have a fairly smooth, weathered surface, but their irregular shape makes them difficult to lay in walks. If you have access to a free source of stone (and a means of transporting it to the building site), pick relatively thin, flat stones with smooth surfaces.

Rubble. Rubble is usually the least expensive stone you can buy at rock yards and patio suppliers. It consists of irregularly shaped stones, usually with sharper edges than fieldstone. Rubble may have been blasted from construction sites, or it may be broken pieces left over from cutting quarried stones. At construction sites, rubble is sometimes free for the hauling. Depending on the type, size, and shape of the stones (and their cost), it may or may not be worth your time and energy to haul them home and try to set them into a walk. Consider your walk requirements carefully before choosing rubble or fieldstone.

Above *For best results, set a dry-laid stone walk in a 2-in.-deep sand bed.*

INSTALLATION TIPS

Stones for dry-laid walks should be at least 1½ inches thick, as thinner stones may break. With stones of consistent thickness, the sand bed is usually 2 inches thick. Stones of varying thickness should be laid on a thicker sand bed. Remove sand as necessary to create a level walk surface. Along walk edges, use larger stones, which aren't so easily dislodged.

Stonework is backbreaking work, so you should not try to do too much in one day or feel pressured to get the job done quickly. Also, it's a good idea to enlist the aid of a strong helper. Even modest-size paving stones can weigh 50 pounds or more.

Estimating Amounts. Quarries and patio suppliers sell natural stone either by the ton or by the cubic yard. Because of the spaces between stones and thickness variations, stones sold by weight or by volume may not cover what they are slated to cover. You'll need to rely on the experience of the supplier to calculate your

needs. Generally, it's best to order 20 to 25 percent more than you think you need to allow for cutting and breakage. Some suppliers will let you return any unused stones. You can also use any extras in other parts of the yard for stepping stones or plant borders.

INTERLOCKING PAVERS

Interlocking pavers are modular concrete units manufactured to fit in a tight pattern. Available in a variety of sizes and shapes, most pavers are 2⅜ to 2½ inches thick, about the same as a standard brick. One type, called a grass paver, has an open-grid shape for planting grass or other ground cover. Grass pavers provide a durable, natural-looking walk surface, and the turf itself helps hold the pavers in place.

For all pavers, check manufacturer's literature for coverage estimates, and buy a few extra for replacement purposes.

Installation. Interlocking pavers are usually butted together and finished with swept-sand joints. Some pavers have small tabs on one side and one end to ensure consistent joint spacing. Laying pavers is much the same job as laying bricks on a sand bed, but check the manufacturer's instructions. (See "Laying Paving Units

Left *Using different size flagstone slabs provides an interesting pattern for this front walkway. Random designs like this often take longer to lay out than consistent patterns.*

Right *Long slabs of quarried slate usually require heavy equipment to transport and set in place.*

in Sand," page 90.) Where soil conditions and climate permit, pavers may be laid directly on well-tamped soil. Depending on the shape of the paver, you may end up with voids or chinks along the edges of the walk. Some manufacturers make special edging pieces to fill the chinks and create a straight edge. Otherwise, you'll have to cut the pavers or fill the voids with mortar to make straight edges.

CONCRETE PATIO BLOCKS

Concrete patio blocks are thinner (usually only 1 inch thick) and therefore less expensive than concrete bricks and interlocking pavers. Patio blocks come in a variety of shapes and colors; the standard size is a 1-foot square that is 1 inch thick. The surface texture is similar to that of concrete building blocks used in foundations, although exposed aggregate surfaces are also common and much more attractive.

As with all molded concrete products, there is little size variation in a given run of concrete patio blocks, and their nominal size is the same as their actual size. Therefore, calculating the number of blocks you need is simply a matter of dividing the total walk area by the area of a single unit. Order 10 percent extra, however, because concrete patio blocks are prone to accidental breakage and don't always split cleanly when you cut them.

Installation. Patio blocks should be set on a highly compacted and well-drained sand-over-gravel base, but you should expect some shifting, sinking, and even breakage due to stress or severe weather conditions. Because concrete patio blocks are only 1 inch thick, there's less area for sand to create an interlocking joint than with concrete bricks or interlocking pavers. To provide a better interlock between the patio blocks, space them ½ inch apart and mix the jointing sand with portland cement in a 1:1 ratio. Sweep the dry mixture into the joints; pack it with a thin wood tamper; then wet it and let it dry for two or three days before using the walk.

Above *Choose flat stones of a consistent thickness when laying a walk directly on the ground.*

Setting Stone Directly on the Ground

Mostly because it is impractical to construct a sand base for thick, irregularly shaped stones, they may be set directly in stable, well-drained soil that isn't subject to frost heave. These walks have topsoil joints, so they are not as formal or as smooth as walks with sand or mortar joints.

POSSIBLE MATERIALS

When setting stone directly on the ground, you'll get the best results using flat stones with a fairly consistent thickness. Another requirement is that the paving be heavy enough so that it can't be dislodged easily. Stones more than 1½ inches thick—including flagstones, fieldstones, and rubble with at least one flat side—and precast concrete stepping stones are good choices.

Most precast concrete stepping stones are 2 inches thick, in square or round shapes, with an exposed-aggregate surface. Others are poured into molds to simulate natural stones; these are referred to as "cultured" stone. You can buy round stones up to 24 inches in diameter;

square stones range from 12 to 48 inches. Space smaller stones 18 to 20 inches apart to accommodate an average stride. Larger stones (2 feet square or larger) can be butted together on firm, tamped soil or sand to form a solid walkway.

LAYING STONE IN THE GROUND

This section describes how to construct a stone walk without a gravel-and-sand base and without edgings. Select a good mix of large and small stones; fill spaces between large stones with small stones.

Outline the Walk. Lay out the edges of the walk, using stakes and string for straight walks or a rope or garden hose for curved walks, as described in "Forming a Curved Walk," page 89. Mark the ground with sand or flour, and remove the sod or loose topsoil within the walk area. Tamp the bottom of the excavation.

Position the Stones. Starting at one end of the walk, select and lay out enough stones to cover about 3 or 4 feet of walkway. Begin with a good-size corner stone. Arrange the stones in a pleasing pattern; try not to group similar sizes and colors. Use smaller stones to fill in between larger ones. Leave ½-inch spaces between stones. **1**

Set the First Stone. Leave one cornerstone in place, but remove those immediately surrounding it. Cut around the stone with a shovel or trowel to mark the outline. **2** Set the stone aside, dig out the area where it will be placed so that the stone rests 1 to 1½ inches above ground level; then set the stone back in position and check it for level. If the stone rocks back and forth, remove it and dig out more dirt until it sits firmly.

If the soil is very hard or rocky and the stone still won't bed properly, dig a slightly deeper hole and backfill with several inches of damp sand to provide a firm base.

Set Remaining Stones. Position the remaining stones in the same manner, leaving at least ½ inch between each stone. Check frequently with a level and straightedge to make sure all the stones are at the same height. **3** Fill the crevices between the stones with soil, and tamp firmly with a ½-inch-thick piece of wood. Spaces between the stones can be planted with ground cover.

Setting Stones in the Ground

TOOLS

- ◪ Work Gloves
- ◪ Round-bottom shovel
- ◪ Flat-bottom shovel
- ◪ Rake
- ◪ Tamper
- ◪ Hammer and cold chisel
- ◪ Level

MATERIALS

- ◪ Flat stones of a consistent thickness

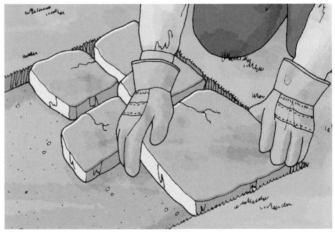

1 *Remove the grass* and topsoil, and place the stones in the pattern you want.

2 *Remove the stones,* and outline the cornerstone. Reset so that is only about 1½ in. above grade.

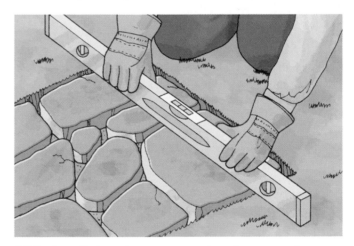

3 *Install the other stones,* using the cornerstone as a guide. Check your work using a level.

Walks on a Gravel-and-Sand Base

Most walks last longer and fare the elements better when built on a base consisting of 2 inches of sand over 4 inches of gravel.

The best gravel for the job is compactible gravel, because you can tamp it to form a well-drained, firm base. Crushed limestone with ¾ inch or smaller stones is ideal for this application. Avoid smooth river-run or pea gravel. When you buy the stone, figure on using 1 cubic yard for every 75 square feet of walk area.

Place a bed of builder's sand on top of the gravel base. The sand helps drain water away from the pavement and makes a smooth, level base that supports individual paving units. When ordering builder's sand, figure on using 1 cubic yard for every 150 square feet of walk area.

Although joints between paving units can be filled with topsoil or mortar, most often dry-laid walks have joints filled with mason's sand. This sand is finer than the builder's sand used for bedding the pavement. The amount of mason's sand needed depends on the size of the joints. For a standard brick walk, you will need a few cubic feet for every 100 square feet of walk area.

PLOTTING AND EXCAVATING THE SUBBASE

Begin by determining the exact width of the walk. On a flat surface, such as a driveway, lay down several courses of the paving pattern you've chosen. Joints should be ⅛ inch or less for sand or ½ inch for topsoil. Measure across the pattern to determine the exact width of the walk. Then cut a piece of wood to that length and use it to check the spacing between the edging or temporary forms when you install them. The following explains how to lay out the path in step-by-step detail.

Locate the Edges of the Walk. At each end of the walk, drive two 1x2 stakes at least 2 feet into the ground to indicate the edges of the walk, and attach strings. Check to make sure that the strings are the same distance apart at both ends. If you want the walk to be square to some other element, such as a sidewalk or the wall of a house, make sure the lines are perpendicular to the element by using the 3-4-5 triangulation method. (See "Using the 3-4-5 Method," page 153.)

Establish the Walk's Height. Mark one stake at each end to indicate the walk's height. In most cases, this will be about 1 inch above ground

Building Forms

Position the layout strings to create a walk that is the width of the strings. If the walk requires forms, drive 2x3 stakes every 2 feet along the walk. For temporary forms, drive the stakes so that their inner edge is outside of the layout lines by the thickness of the form. Add the thickness of the form to the thickness of the edging to determine the location of the stakes.

If the edging will be a ribbon of concrete, drive two rows of stakes as shown in the inset. The outer face of the interior stakes should be inside the layout strings by the width of the form. Set the inner face of the second row of stakes outside the layout string by the width of the edging plus the thickness of the form.

Use galvanized nails or screws to fasten two-by forms to the stakes. Check the placement of the forms with a piece of wood cut to the width of the walk.

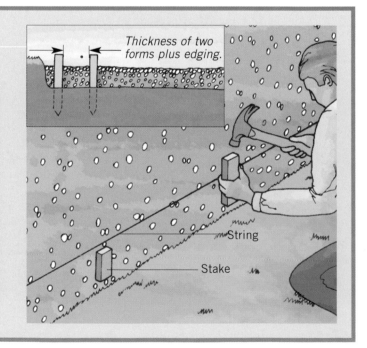

Thickness of two forms plus edging.

String

Stake

Forming a Curved Walk

1. Use a garden hose to lay out the curves. Mark the curves with spray paint or chalk.

2. Dig a trench along the edges with a shovel, deep enough so that the edging will rise above grade.

3. Set edging blocks into the trenches to contain the surface material and prevent erosion.

4. Spread gravel or other finishing material onto the walk in layers, and tamp each layer firmly.

5

Dry-Laid Walks

level. A poured-concrete walk or dry-laid walk with irregularly shaped paving materials, such as flagstones, should be pitched ¼ inch per foot along its width. Mark the walk height on one stake; then use a level to transfer this mark to the opposite stake. Adjust the second mark up or down to establish the pitch, and attach the strings to the stakes.

If drainage is a problem, slope the walk along its length as well. Use a line level to level the strings between the stakes. Measure down the stakes at the far end of the walk to get a ¼-inch-per-foot slope, and attach the strings at this point. (If the walk abuts a sidewalk, the low end of the walk should be level with it.) If the slope between the house and sidewalk is more than about 2 inches per foot, steps may be required. Check with the local building department for code requirements in your area.

Mark the Ground. Mark the location of the walk edges on the ground by sprinkling flour or sand over the strings. Mark the string locations on the stakes, and remove the strings so that they won't interfere when you dig the walk. Make sure the string marks are clear because you will reattach the strings later.

Excavate the Site. Use a pickax and shovel to remove the sod and dig a trench about 1 foot wider than the walk so that you have room to install edging. While digging, reattach the strings periodically to check the depth of the excavation; measure down from your layout strings. The trench needs to accommodate a 4-inch-deep gravel bed and whatever edging you will put on top of it. Use a hand tamper or power tamper to compact the soil in the bottom of the excavation.

Laying Paving Units in Sand

Spread at least 4 inches of compactible gravel in the excavation; tamp it; level it with a rake; then tamp again. **1** Retie the string to the lay-out stakes at the point that marks the top of the walk. Continue adding gravel until an edging set on top of the gravel is level with the layout strings. If you are not installing edging, add and tamp gravel until the distance between it and the strings equals 2 inches plus the thickness of the paving material.

If the walk requires forms or edging, now is the time to install it. (See "Building Forms," page 88.) There are a variety of edge treatments. Some possibilities are shown on page 93. Place the edging material on the gravel, against the forms or aligned with the layout strings. You can adjust the height of the edging by adding sand or gravel as needed.

Add more gravel. Unless you used plastic edging, rake out, compact, and level gravel between the edging until there's just enough space to place the paving material on 2 inches of sand. To help prevent weed growth, place landscape fabric on top of the compacted gravel. **2**

Laying the Walk

TOOLS

- Work Gloves
- Spade
- Rake or hoe
- Hand or mechanical tamper
- Mallet and bedding board
- Broom
- Garden hose
- Brick set for cutting bricks or pavers

MATERIALS

- Landscape fabric
- Sand
- Gravel
- Edging material
- Edging spikes
- Material for forms if needed
- Pavers
- Screed board

1 *After excavating* the walk area, add 2 in. of gravel and tamp. Add another 2 in., and tamp again.

4 *Level the sand* with a screed board. If there are no forms, set up guides for the screed.

5 *Use long spikes* to hold plastic edging in place. Drive the spikes through the edging's perforations.

SPREAD SAND

Shovel builder's sand evenly over the crushed gravel, and spread it with a hoe or rake. **3** With a hose set on fine spray, thoroughly dampen the sand. Fill in any low spots; dampen the filled areas; then tamp the sand firmly. Repeat the process, building up the sand so that the pavers, stones, or bricks will be ¼ to ½ inch higher than the intended walk height, to allow for settling.

While the sand is still moist, pull a notched 1x6 screed board in a zigzag motion along the edging to knock down any high spots in the sand bed and fill in low spots. **4**

After screeding, dampen the sand again with a fine mist. If you are installing plastic edging, now is the time to set it in place. **5**

SET PAVERS

Working from one corner against an edging or string, carefully place the pavement in the desired pattern. **6** Avoid displacing the sand beneath.

Interlocking pavers, such as those shown in this project, are designed to provide automatic spacing as you proceed with the project. **7** To help maintain straight brick or paver courses, mark the walk layout on the forms or edging

5

Dry-Laid Walks

2 **Roll out landscape** *fabric over the entire walk. This will help prevent weed growth.*

3 **Spread about 2 in. of sand** *over the fabric. Use a hoe or rake to smooth out the sand.*

6 **Begin setting the pavers** *by starting in one corner and working out. Set each with a tap of a mallet.*

7 **Continue installing the pavers.** *Be sure to maintain the proper joint distances between pavers.*

(Continued on page 92)

and stretch a string across the marks. Leave a space of 1/16 to 1/8 inch between the paving units for the jointing sand. If you're setting dimensioned stone, arrange the pattern to produce joints of a consistent width (1/2 to 3/4 inch). Joints between irregular flagstones will vary, but try to keep a minimum width of 1/2 inch and a maximum of 1 inch between stones. Check frequently with a level to make sure all units are the same height. Remove any that don't conform or that aren't stable, adding or removing sand as necessary.

After setting several square feet of pavement, run a power tamper over the surface. **8** An-

other option is to lay a 16-inch length of 1x6 on the walk and tap over the entire surface with a hammer or mallet to bed the pavement into the sand. **9**

Avoid standing or kneeling on the sand base or previously laid pavement. If you must kneel on the pavement, lay down a piece of 1/2-inch plywood to distribute your weight.

FILL THE JOINTS

The joints can be filled with sand, topsoil, or mortar. If you choose sand, then spread a thin layer of dry mason's sand evenly over a 5- or 6-foot section of paved walk. With a stiff broom,

Laying the Walk *(Continued from page 91)*

8 **To finish seating the pavers,** *run a power tamper over the entire surface.*

9 **To seat pavers that remain raised,** *lay a board on the surface and pound it with a mallet.*

10 **Spread fine sand** *over the surface, and sweep the sand into the joints between pavers.*

11 **Spray the walk** *to settle the sand into the joints. Repeat steps 10 and 11 if necessary.*

sweep the sand into the cracks between the pavers. Sweep in all directions to fill all the joints completely. **10**

Then lightly spray the walk with water from a garden hose to pack down the sand and wash it off the surface. **11** Do not use a heavy spray, or you will dislodge sand from the joints. Allow the surface to dry; then repeat the process until all the joints are completely compacted.

FILLING WIDE JOINTS

Topsoil or mortar should be used in joints that are wider than ½ inch thick. To fill the joints with topsoil or mortar, lightly hose off the entire walk surface. When all standing water in the joints has disappeared, you can either pack the joints with topsoil and plant grass or a ground cover, or you can mortar the joints, using the method described in "Dry Mortar Method," page 114.

If you installed forms for an edging detail, carefully pull up any temporary forms and shovel gravel along the outside of the edging. Tamp the gravel, and fill the area with a few inches of topsoil. Be sure to cover any permanent stakes. If you used plastic edge restraints, cover them with topsoil, and seed or sod the filled-in area.

WALK EDGING OPTIONS

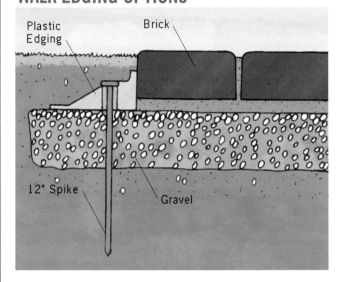

Plastic Edging
Brick
12" Spike
Gravel

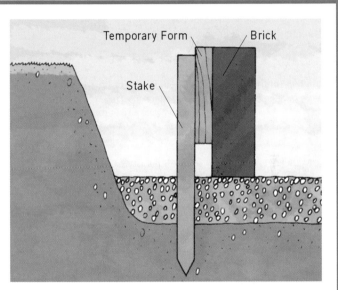

Temporary Form
Brick
Stake

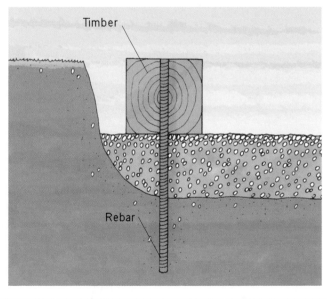

Timber
Rebar

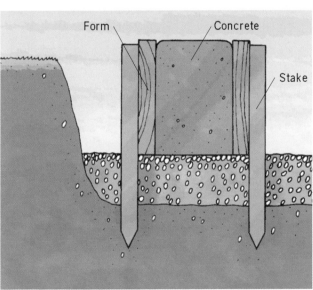

Form
Concrete
Stake

Gallery of Walk Designs

1 Use a loose aggregate material, such as crushed stone or mulch, to soften the lines and edges of straight walks placed in informal setttings.

2 Consider the setting when selecting walk materials. This curving boardwalk is the perfect fit for this water-side garden

3 The width of a walk helps establish a hierarchy in the landscape. Notice how this wide front walk branches off into a narrow path that goes to the back of the house.

4 Edging materials, brick in this case, define the boundaries of a walk and add design interest.

5 Allow plants to spill over the edges of a walk to provide an informal-feeling garden. But for formal gardens, use walks to separate planting areas.

6 Walks complement a number of landscape structures. To add height to a vista with a walkway, include a pergola in the design.

5

6

4

Gallery of Walk Designs

1 Walkways not only help you navigate your yard, they also serve as boundaries, dividing one area from another.

2 Sometimes a walk placed within a well-defined border isn't the best approach. The topography of this yard led to this zigzag pattern.

3 The design of this straight-to-the-door walk is enlivened by the selection of broken pavers set in mortar.

4 One way to enhance a concrete walk is to vary the level and type of aggregate between the different sections.

5 Simple design solutions are often the most elegant, such as this stone path set in a rich green lawn.

Hard Mortar- Bed Walks

Above A mortar-bed walk with mortared joints is a durable and attractive landscape feature.

The most durable type of paved-walk construction involves setting the pavement in a mortar bed over a concrete base. The concrete base keeps the paving units from sinking, buckling, and shifting, and the mortar bed holds the pavement to the concrete. Almost any hard-walk paving material that can be set in sand can be set in mortar. In addition, you can set other materials that would crack if set on a sand bed. These materials include brick and concrete pavers less than 1¼ inches thick, stone less than 1½ inches thick, and all tile.

Mortar-bed walks are well suited to mortared joints because the rigid concrete base minimizes cracking due to ground movement. However, joints may also be filled with sand or soil.

MATERIALS FOR A MORTAR-BED WALK

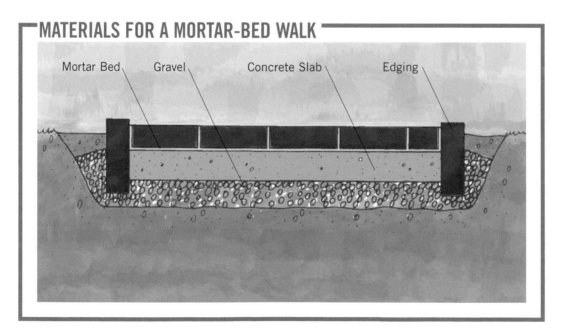

Mortar Bed   Gravel   Concrete Slab   Edging

smart tip

DEALING WITH PAINTED CONCRETE

If an existing walk has been painted or has a slick finish, brush on a solution of muriatic acid and water using a push broom. You can also apply a coat of concrete bonder using a roller. Wear gloves and goggles when using muriatic acid.

Anatomy of a Mortar Walk

As with dry-laid walks, mortar-bed walks should be set on a firm, well drained subbase. Depending on soil conditions, this subbase could be firmly tamped soil, but usually the subbase consists of tamped gravel. A concrete base is placed on the gravel, mortar is spread over the concrete, and the pavement is then bedded in the mortar.

Mortared walks are more difficult and expensive to build than dry-laid walks; however, there's less upkeep as long as the concrete base is structurally sound. You can build a mortar-bed walk over either a new concrete base or an existing concrete walk.

SITE CONDITIONS

A new concrete base should be set low enough so that the finished walk surface will be about 1 inch above grade level. Normally, the concrete is placed on a 4-inch gravel base.

The concrete base should be as wide as the finished walk; lay out a few courses of the paving material on a flat surface (with properly spaced joints) to check the walk width. Place the concrete, and apply a rough-floated or broomed surface to ensure good mortar adhesion. Once the concrete has cured, simply pave over the slab. Edging isn't necessary, although you can add it for aesthetic purposes. If you want to add it, adjust the depth and width of the excavation accordingly.

Using an Existing Walk. You can lay unit masonry over an existing concrete walk, provided the surface is level and stable. Small holes should be patched and leveled with a concrete-patching material. Although the mortar bed will compensate for any minor defects or irregularities in the walk, any cracking or buckling indicates unstable soil, a weak slab, or both. Do not attempt to pave over such walks. It is best to remove the old concrete, and replace the old walk with a new, stable one.

If headroom is limited, consider using stone, ceramic tiles, or split pavers half the thickness of a standard brick.

It's important to clean the surface of an existing walk thoroughly. Remove grease or wax with a commercial driveway cleaner or a solution of 1 part trisodium phosphate (TSP) to 5 parts water. Scrub briskly with a push broom or heavy bristle brush; rinse; and allow to dry.

Above *The crisp mortar joints of this walk complement the sturdy arbor and gate at the end of this walk.*

6

Hard Mortar-Bed Walks

MORTAR MIXES

For most mortar-bed walk projects, it's more convenient to buy ready-mixed mortar, sold by the bag at building suppliers, than to mix your own. The mortar to use, called Type M, is noted for its high compressive strength and water resistance. Type M mortar consists of 1 part portland cement, ¼ part hydrated lime, and 3 parts sand. Local building codes may specify different proportions, depending on your climate. Also, local patio and masonry suppliers can advise you on the best mix for your particular area and application. Lime can stain certain kinds of stone. If your walk will be stone, buy a lime-free mortar mix or substitute fireclay for lime.

Follow the directions on the bag when mixing mortar. The amount of water required depends on the composition of the dry mixture, the width of the mortar joints or mortar bed, the absorption rate of the materials used, and the weather. Because of these many variables, you may have to do some experimentation to achieve the proper mix for your project. Use a wet mix if you are working with brick and concrete patio blocks, because they tend to absorb more water than stone and tile, which require a dry, or stiff, mix.

Tile and gauged stone are either set on a dry bed of mortar, which you wet later, or on latex-portland cement. You can make latex-portland cement mortar by combining the appropriate amount of liquid latex additive to portland cement and sand.

Estimating Mortar Amounts. The quantity of mortar you will need for the mortar bed depends on the size of the walk and the paving material. Generally, large, heavy, or irregularly shaped materials, such as flagstones, require thicker beds than thin and uniform materials, such as split pavers. For estimating purposes, order one 80-pound bag of mortar for every 15 square feet of walk.

The mortar you need to fill the joints depends on the size and number of joints and the size of the paving material. Also, consider the depth of the joints. With 2¼-inch-thick bricks, one 80-

Mixing Mortar

Mix the dry ingredients together in a mortar box or tub to blend them thoroughly.

Add water, and mix. Mortar should be wet but not runny. Peaks should stand on their own.

pound bag of mortar will fill joints for about 160 standard bricks spaced ⅜ inch apart or about 110 standard bricks spaced ½ inch apart.

TOOLS FOR WORKING WITH MORTAR

To mix mortar you'll need a mortar hoe, contractor's wheelbarrow, and mortar box or flat, clean surface, such as a 4- by 4-foot piece of plywood. If you will be mixing a lot of mortar,

Above *The formality of mortar-bed walks makes them good choices for front entry walks.*

it's best to rent a power mixer. Because mortar sets up quickly (usually within 1 hour), you'll be mixing only small amounts at a time (usually 3 cubic feet or less for mortar beds and ½ to 1 cubic foot for joints, depending on how fast you work).

To carry small amounts of wet mortar to the work area, you can use a mason's hawk or make a mortar board from a piece of plywood cut to a convenient size, such as 12 by 12 inches. You will also need several screed boards, to level gravel, concrete, or the mortar bed. The mortar screed board is a length of 2x6 cut a few inches longer than the walk is wide. (Both ends are notched; the depth of the notches usually equals the thickness of the paving material. The others are straight pieces of wood. (See "Using a Screed Board," page 77.)

PREPARING PAVING MATERIALS

Whether they come from a stone yard or your backyard, stones tend to be covered with dirt, dust, and grit. Wash the stones with clear water, because any residue clinging to them will draw moisture from the mortar, weakening the bond. Before setting porous stones, such as sandstone, dampen them so that they don't suck moisture out of the mortar mix. Denser stones, such as Rocky Mountain quartzite, may be set dry.

Brick. Because most face brick absorbs moisture quite readily too, it should be wetted down before setting. Otherwise the bricks will suck moisture out of the mortar base, resulting in a poor bond. You can check the absorbency of the bricks you're setting by putting 20 drops of water in one spot on a sample of the brick. Wait 90 seconds. If the water disappears, spray all of the bricks with a garden hose before you mix the mortar. Continue spraying until water runs out from the brick pile. By the time you get the mortar mixed, the surface water should have evaporated from the bricks, leaving them slightly damp to the touch. Bricks that don't absorb water quickly, such as sealed paver bricks, may be set dry.

Preparing for the Concrete Base

Before you set up the forms and pour the concrete, excavate the site to provide room for a gravel base, a concrete slab, and the paving material. Begin by outlining the walk with stakes and string. Then excavate to a depth that will accommodate a 4-inch gravel base and 1½ inches of concrete and mortar and will place the top of the paving material 1 inch above grade. Remove soil 6 inches beyond each side of the walk to allow room for installing the forms. Tamp the soil firmly to compact it.

INSTALL THE FORMS

The wet concrete is held in place by 2x4 forms, which are removed after the concrete dries. Cut the form boards to length. Align the inside edges of the form boards with the layout strings, and attach the boards to 2x4 stakes with duplex (double-headed) nails or 3-inch galvanized deck screws. Because wet concrete can exert quite a bit of pressure on the forms, space the stakes no more than 4 feet apart. Drive the stakes at least 18 inches into firm ground. **1**

ABSORBENCY TEST

Eye Dropper

Test by placing 20 drops of water in one spot.

---

smart tip

FORMS FOR CURVES
Set up any straight sections of the form with standard lumber, but use ⅛-inch hardboard for the curved sections. To reinforce the bend against the curing concrete, install additional stakes along the outside edge of the form every few inches.

Preparing the Walk

TOOLS	MATERIALS
■ Shovels	■ Lumber for forms
■ Measuring tape	■ Gravel
■ String and stakes	■ Form release agent
■ Work gloves	■ Wire mesh
■ Double-headed nails	■ Stones or bricks
■ Rakes	
■ Wheelbarrows	
■ Screed	
■ Level	
■ Bolt cutters	
■ Tamper	

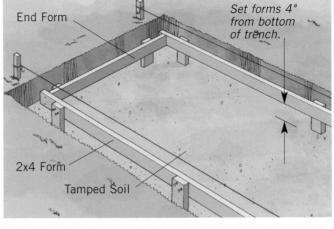

1 *Align the forms* with the layout strings. Set stakes below the top of the form boards.

2 *Add the gravel base;* use the tamper and screed to compact and level the gravel.

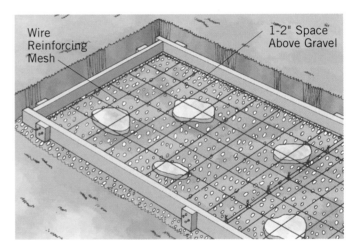

3 *Install the reinforcing* wire mesh so that it falls in the middle of the finished slab.

Make sure the stakes don't protrude above the forms. If more than one form board is needed for either side of the walk, splice the board ends together with a short length of 1x4. At each end of the walk, nail an end form between the side forms and stake each corner securely, as shown.

Add the Gravel. After the forms are placed, spread the gravel evenly in 1-inch layers, tamping each layer firmly before adding the next. **2** Allow some of the gravel to run under the form boards and keep adding gravel until it's ½ inch below the bottom of the formboards. Rake or screed the gravel smooth and level. Brush a commercial form-release agent on the inside of the forms for easy removal.

Add the Wire Mesh. The concrete must be reinforced with wire that has 6- by 6-inch openings. Cut it with heavy wire cutters or large fencing pliers. (You can flatten the unrolled mesh by walking on it.) If more than one piece is required, overlap the pieces by 6 inches, and tie them together with wire. Place stones under the mesh to raise it about 2 inches above the gravel or roughly in the middle of the slab. **3** Avoid walking on the mesh once you've placed it.

6

Hard Mortar-Bed Walks

Pouring the Concrete Bed

Once you've set up the forms and added the base materials, thoroughly hose down the gravel the day before you pour the concrete. If any settling occurs, add more gravel, tamp it, and rescreed it.

If you're mixing and pouring the concrete by yourself, you can work at your leisure, mixing, pouring, and finishing one section of the walk at a time. To make working by yourself easier, put together a movable stop board. Divide the total length of the walk into equal sections; then mark the sections on the form boards. Position the stop board at the end of the first section; secure it with temporary stakes; and pour the concrete up to the board. After finishing the concrete surface, remove the stop board. You can pour the next section right up to the one you just finished or even leave the job for a few days and pick up where you left off.

POURING THE CONCRETE

Because time is limited when you work with concrete, it's important to eliminate potential problems. Provide access for the concrete truck or wheelbarrows. If you think that wheelbarrow traffic might dislodge the form boards, build a

Pouring Concrete

TOOLS

■ Wheelbarrows
■ Containers for mixing concrete
■ Shovels
■ Rakes
■ Hoes
■ Screed

MATERIALS

■ Lumber for concrete forms
■ Expansion strips
■ Concrete

1 *Add expansion strips* where the new walk will abut an existing walk or structure.

3 *Use hoes and rakes* to spread out the concrete. The goal is a smooth surface without air pockets.

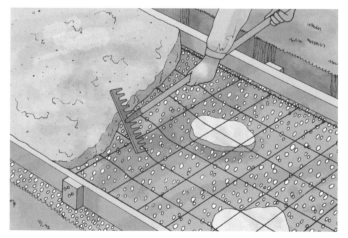

4 *You may need* to adjust the mesh periodically so that it stays in the middle of the slab.

ramp over them. Check the forms to be sure that they are level, spaced correctly, and fastened firmly to the stakes.

Install Expansion Strips. Concrete expands and contracts with the weather, so you need to set expansion strips along the walk every so often. Expansion strips (available at masonry suppliers) consist of a compressible fibrous material that you place between concrete sections. If the walk butts against an existing structure, such as a house foundation, steps, or another walk, you must place an expansion strip between the walk and the existing structure. **1**

2 *When adding concrete* to the excavated area, try to dump one load against the previous load.

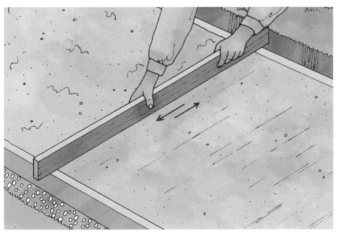

5 *Use a screed board* that spans the width of the pour for additional smoothing.

If the walk is longer than about 40 feet, you'll need to install expansion strips every 8 to 10 feet along the walk (or as required by code). Do not cover the top of the strip with concrete. When the concrete has cured, you can caulk the top of the strip to keep water out.

BEGIN THE POUR

At the end of the walk farthest from the source of the concrete, start placing the material in the forms. If you're using a wheelbarrow to transport the concrete, do not overfill it. Dump the concrete in mounds that extend about ½ inch above the top of the forms. Avoid dumping loads of concrete on top of each other or in separate piles; dump each load against the previous load. **2**

Use a hoe or rake to spread the concrete evenly into the forms, chopping it with the hoe to remove any air pockets. **3** Use the back of the hoe to tamp the concrete into corners and along the edges of the form. If necessary, use a shovel to lift concrete from high spots to fill voids or low spots. After spreading, the concrete fill should be even with, or slightly above, the top edges of the form.

As you pour and spread the concrete, use a hooked prybar, claw hammer, or sturdy rake to pull up the reinforcing mesh so that it remains in the center of the pour. **4** Where necessary, add concrete and tamp to fill any voids under the mesh.

SCREED THE SURFACE

As soon as you've filled 4 or 5 feet of walkway, use a screed board to strike off excess concrete. Select a straight 2x4 approximately 1 foot longer than the width of the forms. Starting at the back end of the pour, place the screed board firmly on the form boards, and pull it toward you in a side-to-side sawing motion. **5** Fill any hollow spots with more concrete, and rescreed, always pulling the screed in the direction of the unscreeded area. Use a hoe to pull away any concrete that builds up in front of the screed board. Do not reuse any concrete that spills outside the forms, because it will be contaminated with soil.

6

Hard Mortar-Bed Walks

Curing Strategies

You must keep concrete moist as it cures. If the concrete dries out too quickly, hairline cracks can develop or the surface develops a chalky residue.

Apply a fine spray of water. Too much pressure can wash out the concrete finish.

Commercial curing compounds that you apply with a roller can retard moisture loss.

Cover the walk with plastic sheeting to keep moisture from escaping. Overlap sheet edges.

Finishing the Concrete Surface

Concrete beds need either a rough-floated or broomed surface to ensure good mortar adhesion. You'll give the bed an initial floating and edging, then play a waiting game before finishing the surface. The amount of waiting time depends on climatic conditions—wind, humidity, temperature—and the type of mix used. As a general rule, you can start finishing the concrete as soon as the water sheen disappears from the surface and the concrete is hard enough to make a thumbprint about ¼ inch deep. If you start too soon, you'll notice excess water bleeding to the surface, which will weaken the slab. If you wait too long, the concrete won't smooth out at all, and you'll be stuck with the surface you have.

ROUGH-FLOAT THE SURFACE

Right after screeding the surface, float the concrete to level it and embed any aggregate below the surface. For most walks, floating is done with a darby, although very wide walks will require a bull float, which has a long handle so that you can reach the middle of the slab. Swing the darby in an arcing motion along the length of the walk. **1** As you work, tilt the leading edge of the tool slightly upward to avoid digging into the wet concrete. Do not apply too much pressure. Also, do not overwork the surface. When water starts to appear on the surface, you are done. If too much water rises to the surface, remove it by dragging a garden hose or heavy rope over the walk, directing the water over the sides of the forms.

Edge the Slab. Immediately after floating the concrete with the darby, insert a pointed trowel between the forms and the concrete, and slide the tool along the forms to separate them from the concrete. **2** Repeat the edging process after each smoothing operation.

Apply the Finish. Once the concrete is "thumbprint hard," you can rough-trowel the surface by making one or two passes with a wood float. **3** If desired, you can run a broom across the surface to create a rougher surface for the mortar.

CURING CONCRETE

There are several ways to keep concrete moist, which is the key to the curing process. (See "Curing Strategies," opposite.) The most common method is to apply fine spray to the surface of the concrete. Coverage should be light, yet thorough. Keep the slab moist for about one week; be sure to check the slab several times a day. Reduce evaporation by covering the surface with plastic sheeting. Another option is to the concrete with water-saturated burlap or canvas. But be sure to keep the covering wet during the curing period by adding water periodically. This is especially important during hot, dry weather.

If the temperature drops below 50 degrees, continue curing for another 3 to 7 days. If you expect freezing weather, cover the slab with 6 to 12 inches of straw or hay covered with a tarp or plastic sheet. After about 10 days, remove the forms and backfill along the edges of the walk.

Finishing Concrete

TOOLS
- Darby
- Bull floats
- Trowels
- Wood float
- Stiff-bristle broom
- Paint roller (optional)

MATERIALS
- Water from garden hose
- Plastic sheeting or canvas
- Concrete curing compound (optional)

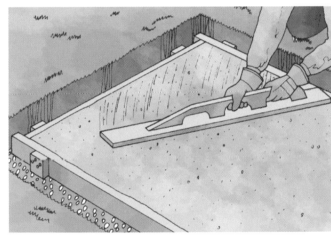

1 **Work with a darby** to level the concrete further. Tilt the leading edge up, so it doesn't catch the work.

2 **Run a trowel** between the forms and the concrete. This will help in removing the forms later.

3 **Use a wood float** to create a rough surface on the concrete. You can also use a stiff-bristle broom.

Setting the Walk

Once the concrete bed has cured, you can begin setting the mortar bed on it. Here we show how to install a brick path, but you can use any masonry material. If you are working with irregularly shaped stones, plan on spending a little more time deciding which stone goes where.

SET FORMS

For a brick walk, install bricks on edge. **1** You can also install a removable form. At this stage, the form or edging is there to contain the walk materials. For a wood form, install temporary 2x4 forms on either side (but not on top of) the concrete slab. Set one side to a height that equals the thickness of the mortar bed and pavement. Set the other side higher to pitch the walk for water runoff. The pitch should equal ⅛ inch per foot of width.

Do a dry run with the paving material. **2** This will help you establish a pattern and tell you how much cutting of the paving material is required. To space bricks, use ⅜- or ½-inch wood strips and determine the size and number of cut

Left Use edging to form a simple grade-level border, or use it to create a slightly raised planting area.

Finishing the Walk

TOOLS

- Wheelbarrow
- Measuring tape
- Work gloves
- Hammer
- Rake
- Mason's and notched trowels
- Striking tool
- Grout bag

MATERIALS

- String and line level
- Exterior-grade paving bricks
- Other paving materials
- Lumber for form and stakes
- Mortar mix

1 *Apply edging* to hold the field materials in place. Here bricks are set on edge.

PROTECT YOUR LAWN
Running a heavy wheelbarrow full of concrete, stones, or bricks back and forth across your yard can ruin the lawn. Often the only recourse is to reseed or resod the entire area after installing the walk. To protect the grass and grounds around the work site, mix concrete and cut and store materials on tarps on the driveway. To transport materials, lay a series of planks and plywood sheets along the intended supply route. This will save wear and tear on the lawn, and you will find it easier to push a heavy wheelbarrow over the wood than through soft soil.

bricks necessary. Between irregular stones, joints should be between ½ and 1½ inches wide. Joints for dimensioned stones should be no more than 1 inch wide.

THE MORTAR BED

Prepare the mortar bed. Hose down a few feet of the slab. Mix enough mortar to cover a small section, and pour it on the slab. Use a wetter mix for brick and a drier mix for heavy paving materials, such as flagstones. The mortar bed should be at least ½ inch thick for bricks and dimensioned stone and at least 1 inch thick for paving of varying thickness, such as flagstone.

Level the mortar with a screed. As your working speed increases, you can mix and screed mortar to cover larger areas. Use the notched trowel to create furrows in the mortar. **3** This leads to a better bond between the mortar and the walk material. If you are setting flagstones, furrow the screeded mortar bed with the edge of your trowel.

2 *Lay a dry run* of the field material you have chosen. Adjust bricks to reduce cuts.

3 *Trowel mortar* onto a small area. Rake it out with a notched trowel.

(Continued on page 112)

SETTING THE WALK

Starting at one corner, gently set the paving units into the mortar bed with a slight twisting motion. **4** Use wood spacers to establish the joint widths.

If you're setting bricks with sand joints, butt each brick carefully against its neighbor to keep mortar from squeezing up between the joints. If you are using stone, fill any depressions or hollows on the underside with mortar before setting. If the stones vary in thickness, set the thickest stones first; then set thinner ones to the same height by adding mortar beneath them.

Bed bricks in the mortar with a firm tap from a trowel handle. To bed stones, use a rubber mallet. Use a level to make sure all units are at the same height. If one is too low, too high, or out of level, gently pry it up with a prybar and add or remove mortar as needed.

FILL THE JOINTS

Mix a batch of mortar that is thin enough to pour, but not too soupy or watery. If you are mixing your own ingredients, combine 1 part cement to 3 parts sand. Put the mortar in a grout bag, and force mortar into the joints between the bricks. **5** If you don't have a grout bag, scoop some mortar into a coffee can, bend the can rim slightly to form a spout, and pour the mortar into the joints. Work carefully to avoid getting mortar on the walk surface. If you do spill some, clean up as you go along rather than waiting for it to harden completely.

Tooling the Joints. Use a trowel to strike the mortar flush to the surface and remove any excess mortar. Continue filling and striking until all joints are filled, including any gaps between the edge stones and the forms.

Before the mortar hardens completely, you can tool the joints with a piece of dowel or jointing tool to produce a slightly concave surface. **6** To use the tool, draw it over the joints while applying light pressure. Avoid making deep, recessed joints, which will trap dirt and water and make a rougher walking surface.

Finishing Touches. Remove excess mortar using a trowel. **7** Several hours after tooling, brush off any mortar crumbs with a whisk broom, then lightly scrub the walk surface with a damp sponge or wet burlap sack to remove any mortar smears.

Once the mortar has set (about one week), any remaining mortar haze can be removed by applying a light solution of TSP (½ cup per gallon of water) and scrubbing with a stiff brush or broom. Rinse thoroughly with clear water.

Finishing the Walk *(Continued from page 111)*

4 *Set the bricks in the mortar with a slight twist. Use a guide string to keep the bricks aligned.*

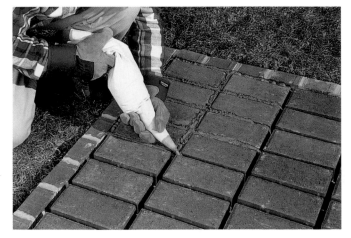

5 *To fill joints, use a grout bag. This method cuts down on mortar spills on the bricks.*

smart tip

CUTTING BRICKS BY HAND

It is easier to use a circular saw with a masonry blade to make complicated cuts. But for only a few simple cuts, make them by hand. Mark a cut line on the brick, allowing for the joint space, and score the line with a chisel. To make the cut, tap a brick set placed over the line lightly before delivering a heavy blow.

Right Even if you plan a complex brick pattern, laying out the bricks in a dry run will help you keep the number of cuts to a minimum.

6 *Draw a striking tool* over the joints between the bricks, creating a slightly concave finish.

7 *Strike excess mortar* from the surface of the bricks using a trowel.

Dry Mortar Method

Rather than mixing a batch of mortar and pouring it into the joints, many stonemasons use a dry-mortar method to save time and labor. If you live in a warm climate, where freeze-thaw conditions are not a concern, you can use this method to fill joints between bricks, blocks, or stones. Here's how to proceed.

1. Mix and spread the mortar. After cleaning the walk surface, mix 1 part portland cement with 3 parts sand, or use bags of premixed mortar. Spread the dry mortar evenly over the walk area; then sweep it into the joints using a stiff broom or stiff-bristle brush.

2. Pack mortar in the joints. Use a short piece of wood to pack the dry mixture firmly into the joints. Sweep in more dry mix, if necessary, and continue packing the joints until the mortar in the joints is flush with the surrounding paving material.

3. Moisten the joints. Set the nozzle on a garden hose to spray fine mist and dampen the mortar. Gently soak the joints, being careful not to flush the mortar out. Don't allow pools of water to form. Over the next hour, keep the surface moist by periodically misting with a hose.

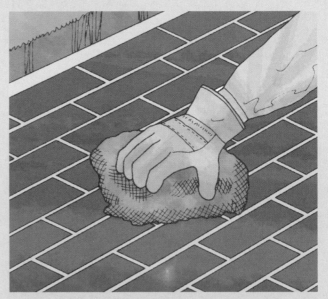

4. Finish the joints, and clean off excess. When the mortar hardens slightly, you either can tool concave joints with a convex jointer or strike the joints flush with a trowel. When the mortar dries, clean the excess off the stones with a damp piece of burlap.

Ceramic and Stone Tile

Tile—either stone or ceramic—lends a formal look to a walk and often is used to make an indoor-outdoor connection. Tile is expensive, however, and many kinds aren't suited for outdoor use. Generally, climatic conditions in your area will dictate which outdoor tiles will be carried at local tile dealers and stone yards.

Unless you're tiling an existing concrete walk, choose the tile first, then lay out the walk based on the tile size. Most tile dealers will loan you a few samples for this purpose. Sizes for square tiles range from 4 inches to 24 inches; other shapes include rectangles, hexagons, octagons, and curved ogee profiles. Ceramic floor tiles usually look best with mortared joints spaced ⅜ to ½ inch apart. Stone tiles can be either butted together with swept-sand joints or spaced for mortared joints.

Although most ceramic and stone tiles are extremely dense, they are also brittle and thin (⅜ to ¾ inch thick), so they require a perfectly smooth, flat, and sturdy concrete base. Rather than being set in mortar, tiles are set in special thin-set cement tile adhesive. Consult the tile dealer or manufacturer for the appropriate type of adhesive for your particular project.

SUITABLE TYPES OF TILE

In most outdoor situations you'll want a tile that doesn't absorb too much water—one that can go through the freeze-thaw cycle without cracking. You'll also want tiles that won't become slippery when wet. Some tile manufacturers use a labeling system devised by the International Standards Organization that makes it clear which tiles are best. A snowflake on the box indicates that the tile is freeze-thaw resistant. A footprint means the tile stands up well to foot traffic, and a hand means the tile is for walls only. Without the labels, however, it's very hard to tell from the box whether a given tile is good for outdoor use. Fortunately, some categories of tile have proven themselves for outdoor use. Unglazed quarry tile, unglazed pavers, and gauged stone are all tiles that work well outdoors.

Unglazed Quarry Tile. This category includes any hard, red-bodied ceramic floor tile of consistent dimensions, not less than ⅜ inch thick. Most are vitreous (glossy in appearance) or semivitreous. The tile body (called the bisque) is usually a deep brick red, although pigments may be added to produce other colors, usually earth tones or pastels.

Unglazed Pavers. All tiles that are not classified as quarry tiles are called unglazed pavers, although the terms are sometimes used interchangeably. Pavers range from impervious porcelain varieties to nonvitreous clay. Use the densest you can find. These pavers are usually uniform in size and dimension and come in a wide variety of colors and surface textures.

Cement-Bodied Tile. As the name implies, these tiles are made of cement. Extruded cement-bodied tiles are extremely dense and offer strong resistance to wear. Tiles made for outdoor use are treated with a sealer that must be reapplied periodically.

Gauged Stone. Slate, marble, and granite come as gauged stone tiles. They are cut to precise shapes (squares or rectangles) and sizes, and they're ground to uniform thickness. The surface may be left natural or machine-polished to a high sheen. Set much like ceramic tile, gauged stone is extremely expensive and is used for interior floors, walls, and countertops. However, you can use it to make an indoor-outdoor connection, such as extending a stone floor in a foyer out to a front porch. For outdoor use, avoid stones with smooth, slick surfaces.

Cutting Tiles. If you have a lot of tiles to cut, it's best to rent a tile saw. If you need to cut only a few tiles, use a hacksaw with a carbide-grit blade to make a groove in the face of the tile about ¹⁄₁₆ inch deep along the cut line. (Very thick tiles may require a second cut on the backside.) Place the tile over a wood dowel or length of heavy insulated wire, and press down sharply on either side to snap the tile. (See "How To Cut Tiles," page 116.)

6

Hard Mortar-Bed Walks

Setting Tiles in Mortar

Setting tiles and gauged stone in mortar over a concrete walk is done pretty much the same way as with bricks or patio blocks. Square tiles can be laid in a jack-on-jack or running-bond pattern. These tiles also can be laid diagonally. Fill in the edges with triangular pieces that you cut using the score-and-snap method described previously.

PREPARE THE SURFACE

Existing concrete walks should be cleaned thoroughly to remove all grease, oil, wax, and other contaminants. Use a solution of 1 cup TSP to 1 gallon of water. You should patch and level small holes with a concrete patching material. Treat slick-troweled or painted surfaces with muriatic acid or concrete bonder.

Tile and gauged stone are laid in a either dry-set mortar or latex-portland cement. Check with the tile manufacturer for the appropriate product and application requirements. To set a wet coat of mortar, first apply a ¼-inch bond coat of mortar over the entire walk with a flat trowel and allow it to dry. **1** Then apply a second coat with a ½-inch notched trowel, on which you'll set the tile. Ideally, the mortar should be applied on a warm, mild day (about 65° and out of direct sunlight to prevent the mortar from setting up too quickly). Spread only as much mortar as you can cover with tile before the mortar sets up— in about a half hour.

LAY THE TILES

Starting at one end of the walk, lay the tiles in the chosen pattern, with open (⅜- or ½-inch) joints. To ensure even joints, make a spacer stick by nailing 4-inch lengths of wood lath to a piece of 1x4. Position the pieces of lath on the 1x4 so that they fit in the joints between two tiles. **2** Use a 4-foot level or a 2-foot level placed atop a straightedge to make sure all the tiles are even.

Use a rubber mallet or a hammer and wood block to bed the tiles into the mortar. Tap lightly over the center of each tile. Recheck the tiles for alignment and level. **3**

Prepare a mortar mixture of 3 parts sand to 1 part portland cement, or use a premixed bagged grout. Add water until the mix is easy to pour but not too soupy. To pour the mortar, use a large can with a bent rim to form a spout. **4** You can also use a rubber float to force mortar into the joints.

After the mortar sets up (which takes about 15 to 20 minutes), remove any excess mortar with a flat trowel and wipe off the tile surface with a coarse, damp cloth. Then tool the joints. **5** Most installations look best with a slightly concave joint, which you can make with a jointing tool or a short length of dowel or copper tubing. After striking the joints with a trowel, clean the tile surface again to remove mortar smears. Dried mortar film or haze remaining on the surface can be removed with a commercial tile cleaner. After the mortar joints are thoroughly dry (which can sometimes take two to six weeks of warm weather), you can apply a clear tile sealer to protect the tile from stains and weather. Consult your tile dealer for the appropriate product to use in exterior applications.

HOW TO CUT TILES

Groove

Wood Dowel

Carbide-Grit Blade

Above *Be sure to select tile that is suitable for outdoor use.*

Setting a Tile Walk

TOOLS

- Garden hose
- Notched trowels
- Pointed trowels
- Tile saw
- Mortar hoe
- Level
- Rubber mallet
- Striking tool
- Rubber float

MATERIALS

- Lumber for jig
- Tile
- Tile adhesive
- Tile spacers
- Mortar or grout

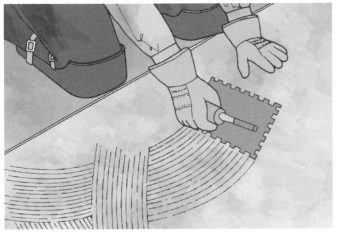

1 *Apply thinset adhesive to the concrete slab. It may be necessary to apply two coats.*

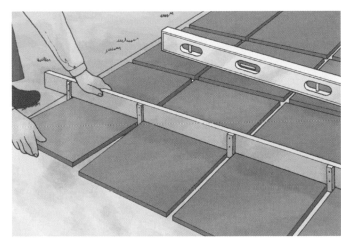

2 *Place tiles in the adhesive. Make a jig from a 1x4 and wood lath to maintain spacing.*

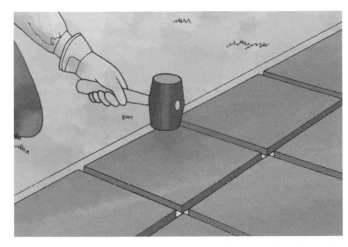

3 *Bed tiles by tapping with a rubber mallet. Tap the center of each tile lightly.*

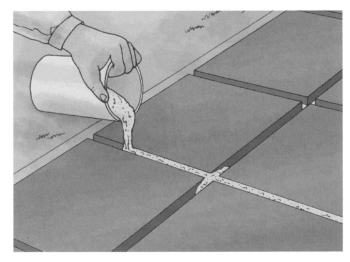

4 *Pour mortar into the tile joints. Use a can with a bent spout or a grout bag.*

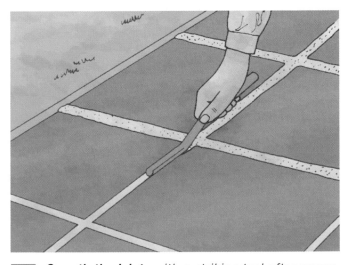

5 *Smooth the joints with a striking tool after removing any mortar from the tile surface.*

6

Hard Mortar-Bed Walks

Building Steps

Above Even this "rough" stone stair has a safe tread and riser relationship.

Below For comfort and ease of use, make your steps as wide as the walks they connect.

If the ground level of your walk changes dramatically or if your patio is terraced into the side of a hill, steps or ramps need to be part of your design. While both require a little thought, some math, and careful layout, you'll find that actual construction is simple.

Exterior steps are generally less steep than interior steps: the step itself is wider, and the rise between steps is smaller, making the steps easier to navigate in bad weather. The exact design of your steps or ramp will depend on the terrain, but all steps have certain things in common.

Step Design

Steps must be wide enough to accommodate the traffic they have to handle. Steps 4 feet wide are usually adequate for one person to stroll comfortably. Two people walking abreast need a walk 5 to 6 feet wide. Steps in the middle of walks should be the same width as the walk.

Steps leading to entries, decks, and patios should be wide enough to complement the scale of their surroundings. Build narrow steps for a small patio: they'll look proportionate and will easily handle the traffic. A large patio, on the other hand, may call for steps wider than strictly necessary. The extra width helps accommodate the occasional crowd and helps keep the steps in scale with the surroundings.

Tread/Riser Relationships. All steps have two critically important dimensions. The tread depth is measured from the front to the back of the tread—the part of the step on which you walk. Technically, tread depth is called the unit run. The height of the individual step is equally important and is called the unit rise. Typically, the higher the unit rise, the shallower the tread. As a rule of thumb for exterior steps, the combined length of one tread and two rises should be 25 to 27 inches.

The maximum rise between any two steps should be the amount most people are comfortable stepping up—between 5 and 7 inches. This leaves a tread depth of between 11 and 17 inches. Many landscape designers believe that the best tread/riser proportion for garden steps is a 15-inch tread with a 6-inch riser.

Landings. Where a flight of steps is at right angles to a walk or driveway, there should be at least a 3-foot landing between the steps and the walk or drive. If a door or gate opens toward a landing or porch, the landing should be the width of the door plus at least 3 feet. Landings should be the same width as the treads.

FINDING THE RUN AND RISE
Before you can figure tread/riser relationships, you need to compute the total rise and the total run. The total rise is the height between the lowest and highest levels of the stairs. The run is the horizontal distance from one end of the stairs to the other.

If the steps run from a walk to a patio or deck, you get the rise by measuring the height of the structure. If the steps go up a hillside, drive a tall stake into the ground at what will be the bottom of the stairs and a short stake at the top of the stairs. Each stake should be plumb, and the tops should be at about the same height. Tie a string to the upper stake at ground level, then tie the string to the lower stake. Level the string with a line level, and measure the distance at the tall stake from the ground to the string: this distance equals the rise. To find the run, measure the horizontal distance between the stakes.

Determining Tread and Riser Sizes. Once you know the rise and run, you can figure out the tread and unit rise. To determine the unit rise, divide the total rise by the potential number of steps. Remember, the ideal unit rise is between 5 and 7 inches. If your answer is outside this range, adjust the number of steps. If, for example, the total rise is 39 inches and you have 5

PLANNING STEPS
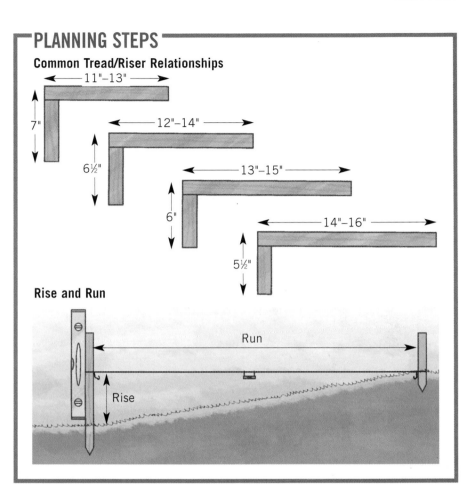

Common Tread/Riser Relationships

Rise and Run

steps in mind, you'd need a riser height of $7^{13}/_{16}$ inches (39÷5=7.8)—too big for outdoor use. Six steps would give you a riser height of 6½ inches (39÷6=6.5), well within the right range.

Once you know the unit rise, calculate tread depth. Remember, the tread depth plus twice the unit rise should be between 25 and 27 inches. Twice the riser height in our example is 13 inches; subtracting that from 25 and then from 27 tells you that the treads should be between 12 and 14 inches deep). Choose the depth that will give you the proper run.

If the rise and run won't work out to something that fits the formula, you usually have flexibility about where the top and the bottom of the steps will be located. If necessary you can adjust the total run to create a stairway that has a comfortable rise-and-run ratio.

smart tip

SOD FOR PATCHING
Before excavating, undercut the sod with a spade and roll it up. You can use the extra sod to patch bare spots elsewhere in the lawn.

Wood Steps

On steep or irregular slopes or severe grade changes, raised steps can often bridge the grade change with little or no excavation or grading required. On gentle slopes you can outline each step by laying landscape timbers directly on the ground and filling the spaces between them with smooth stones, bricks, poured concrete, or other suitable walk materials.

STEPS ON GRADE

The steps shown below are supported by a notched wooden stringer to which the treads are nailed. The stringer lays directly on the same type of sand-and-gravel base that supports the rest of the walk. Concrete footings at each end of the steps anchor them in place.

BUILDING THE STEPS

Drive a stake at each of the four corners of the steps, and connect them with string to locate the steps on the ground.

To build a support for the bottom end of the stringers, excavate a 10-inch-deep trench that extends about 6 inches beyond the sides of the steps. Fill the trench with a 6-inch layer of gravel, and tamp it. Then install a 2x4 form; fill the trench with concrete; and level the concrete by pulling a screed across the forms. Before the concrete dries, insert anchor bolts with hex-head nuts to hold steel framing angles. **1** The space between the framing angles should equal the space between the stringers. Install a second footing to support the top end of the stringers. If you are installing a concrete walk or patio at the bottom of the stair, either one can serve as a footing for the stair.

Lay Out the Stringers. Stringers are usually made from 2x12 stock. Lay out a single stringer with a framing square before making any cuts. After you cut the first stringer, use it as a template for cutting the second.

Begin your layout with your framing square. With tape, mark the length of a riser on the outside of one arm. With another piece of tape, mark the width of the tread on the outside of

the other arm. Put the framing square at the top end of the stringer board, as shown. With a pencil, mark a tread and the first riser. **2**

Mark the Rest of the Steps. Reposition the square, as shown. First, position the tape indicating the tread rise on the edge of the board at the top of the first step. Then position the tape indicating the tread width with the edge of the board. Draw lines along the square to mark the riser and tread. Repeat for the other steps. **3**

Extend the line for the top riser, as shown, to mark the top end of the stringer. As laid out, the bottom step will be larger than the others by the thickness of the stair tread. Measure up a tread thickness from the existing layout line, and draw a new line. Cut along this line to mark the bottom of the stringer. **4**

Cut along the layout lines with a circular saw, but do not cut past the line for the adjoining riser or tread. Finish the cuts with a handsaw. Use the first stringer as a template to mark the second stringer, and cut it out. **5** If necessary, notch the stringer to fit around the footing at the top of the hill. Attach the stringer to the bolts in the concrete using angle brackets.

Add at least 1 inch to the width of the tread to create a tread that overhangs the one below it. Cut the treads from two-by lumber. Nail or screw the treads in place with 10d galvanized nails or 3-inch deck screws. Predrill nail and screw holes to avoid splitting the wood. Leave a ¼- to ½-inch space between treads to facilitate drainage and to allow for wood expansion. (Butt pressure-treated lumber.)

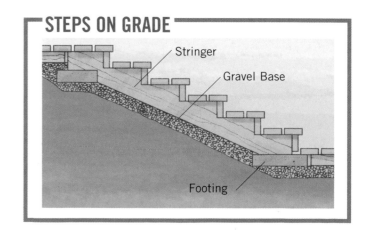

STEPS ON GRADE

Stringer

Gravel Base

Footing

Building Wood Steps

TOOLS

- Shovels
- Gravel tamper
- Picks
- Concrete mixing tools
- Circular saw
- Framing square
- Handsaw
- Hammer
- Power drill/driver

MATERIALS

- Gravel
- Concrete
- Anchor bolts
- Steel framing angles
- Lumber for stringers
- Lumber for risers and treads

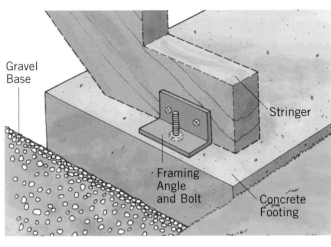

1 *Place anchor bolts* in the wet concrete while you are pouring the footing.

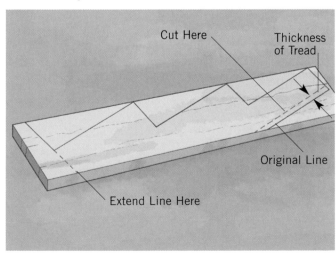

2 *Mark the rise* on the framing square; mark the unit run on the other arm.

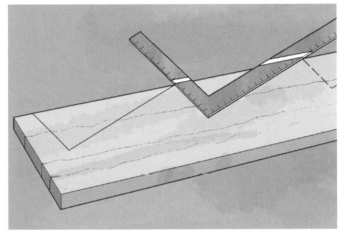

3 *Move the marked* framing square down the stringer to mark the other notches.

4 *Mark the bottom* of the stringer to adjust for the thickness of the stair treads.

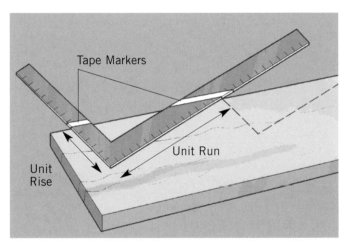

5 *Use the cut stringer* as a template to mark and cut the other stringer.

Landscape Steps

If your steps will be along a grade, you can often build them directly on the ground without a stringer. The steps shown here will work well on a hillside where the run equals 24 to about 32 inches per foot of rise.

Compute the Rise and Run. First, measure the overall rise and run of your steps. The riser height is determined by the thickness of a landscape tie—6 inches. **1** Divide the rise by 6 and round off to the nearest whole number to determine the number of steps. Divide the run by the number of steps to determine tread depth. For a comfortable stairway, the tread should be between 13 and 15 inches deep. Outline the stairs with string and stakes. **2**

Excavate the First Step. Start at the bottom of the stairs. Dig a trench for the first riser, which should be little more than a shallow groove in the ground. Dig trenches for the side timbers, which need to be long enough to extend 6 inches past the riser of the next step. Check to make sure the trenches are level. **3**

Measure and cut the side timbers to length. Bore ½-inch holes 2½ inches from each end of all three timbers. Put the riser in place, and remove and add soil as needed to level it.

Building Landscape Steps

TOOLS

- Tools and Materials
- Measuring tape
- Line level
- Shovels
- Picks
- Handheld sledge
- Screed
- Stiff-bristle broom
- Garden hose

MATERIALS

- Lumber for stakes
- Landscape timbers
- Gravel
- Sand
- Bricks
- Rebar and landscape spikes
- Mason's sand

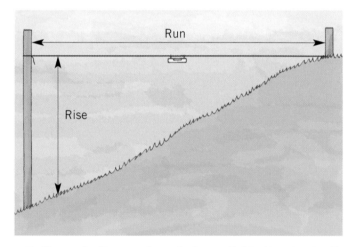

1 *Compute the number of steps: divide the rise by 6 in. (the height of a landscape tie).*

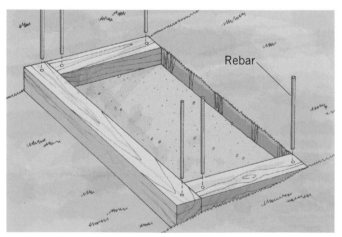

4 *Drill pilot holes, and drive 18-in.-long sections of rebar or landscape stakes through the timbers.*

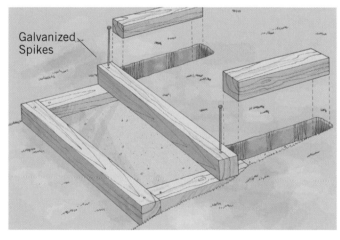

5 *Dig trenches for the next riser and timbers. Use spikes to attach timbers to the level below.*

Anchor it to the ground by driving 18-inch lengths of #4 (½-inch) rebar or landscape spikes through the holes and into the ground. **4**

Set the side timbers in place, and level and anchor them, too.

Dig a trench for the next riser, and trench back into the hill for the sides, as before. Set the riser roughly in place. Measure from the front of the first riser to locate the second riser precisely. The riser is attached to the side timbers below it with 12-inch galvanized spikes. Drill a pilot hole about 5 inches into the riser, and spike the riser to the side timbers below it. **5**

When you install the top step, cut the side timbers 6 inches shorter than the ones on the lower steps—these timbers do not need the extra length, as no further stairs will be resting on them.

Backfill with Gravel and Sand. The bricks sit on a bed of 2-inch bed of gravel toped by a 2-inch bed of sand. Use a screed to level the sand.

Place the bricks. Leave ¹⁄₁₆- to ⅛-inch joints between the bricks. **6** On the top step, lay the bricks, then trench behind them for a timber that will enclose the back of the step.

Fill the joints with mason's sand following the directions outlined in "Laying Paving Units in Sand," page 90. **7**

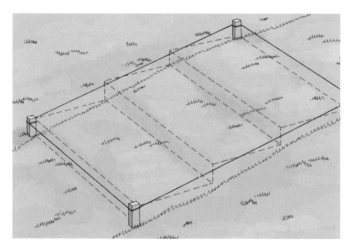

2 *Mark the location* of the steps by driving stakes at the corners and stretching string between them.

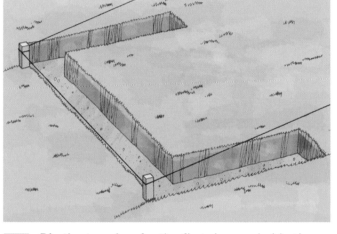

3 *Dig the trenches* for the first riser and side timbers. The sides must support the next riser.

6 *Add gravel and sand* to the steps. Bed bricks by tapping a 1x6 placed on the surface.

7 *Sweep mason's sand* into joints. Wet area with a light spray from a garden hose.

Concrete Steps

Concrete steps are durable and work well as garden steps to traverse slopes in the landscape. A broomed surface provides good traction even when the steps are wet.

When building concrete steps, dig a flat-bottomed trench into the hillside and line it with gravel. Then build a step-shaped form that molds the concrete into one long stairway.

Concrete garden steps require a footing at the bottom. If there are more than three steps, you'll need a footing at the top as well. The footing should be at least 2 feet deep, or in areas where freezing occurs, six inches below the frost line. Pour the footing before the steps, and stick reinforcing bars in it that extend up to tie the steps to the foundation. For more on foundations, see Chapter 9, "Footings for Walls," beginning on page 146.

DETERMINE RUN AND RISE

Drive a stake in the ground at the top of the grade, about where you want the top of the steps to be. Hook your tape measure over the stake, and pull the tape out until you reach the bottom of the grade. **1** Stop at an even number if you can—say, 8 feet. Drive a longer stake into

Building Concrete Steps

TOOLS

- Line level
- Shovels and picks
- Stakes and layout string
- Framing square
- Measuring tape
- Circular saw
- Hammer and nails
- Double-headed nails
- Power drill-driver and screws
- Screed
- Darby
- Edger
- Wooden float

MATERIALS

- Lumber for forms
- Concrete
- Rebar
- Lumber for braces
- Clean masonry rubble
- Wire mesh

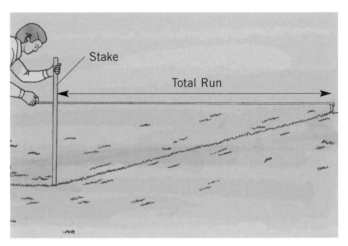

1 *To determine the run,* stretch a level string between stakes at the top and bottom of the hill.

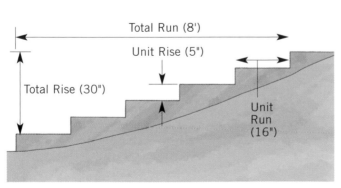

3 *Divide the rise* and then the run by the number of steps to find a safe riser/tread relationship.

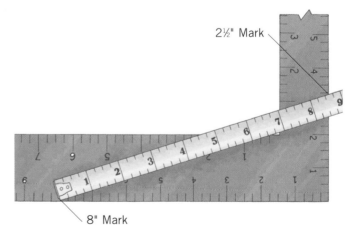

4 *To estimate form length,* use a framing square and a tape measure.

the ground at this point. Use a level to check that the stake is plumb.

Tie string to the uphill stake. Mason's twine is best. Make sure the string is attached to the uphill stake at ground level. Stretch the string tautly to the downhill stake, and put a line level on it. Adjust the string at the downhill side until it is level. When it is, mark where the string crosses the downhill stake. Now measure from the ground to the mark to get the total rise. **2**

Determine the Unit Rise and Run. As mentioned, the ideal riser height (unit rise) for outdoor stairs is 6 inches. If, for example, the total rise is 30 inches, you need five steps (30÷6=5). Dividing the total run of 96 inches by five steps gives you a tread depth (unit run) of 19.2 inches. That's too deep for a comfortable stride.

Here's what happens if you try six steps: 96 inches divided by six steps equals 16 inches for the unit run, well within the acceptable range. With a total rise of 30 inches, six steps would give you 5-inch risers; 5 inches is a small riser, but still within the acceptable range. **3** For more information, see "Tread/Riser Relationships," page 120.

Calculate the Side-form Lengths. Make your side forms from 2x12s. Here's a quick way to use your framing square and tape measure to determine how long the boards need to be.

Using a scale of 1 inch equals 1 foot, measure from the framing square's blade to its tongue to find the length of the form board. The example stairway has a total run of 96 inches—8 feet—so start measuring from the 8-inch mark on the blade. The example stairway's total rise is 30 inches—2½ feet—so measure up to the 2½-inch mark on the square's tongue. The measurement on the tape measure is about 8½ inches. Since lumber is sold in 2-foot increments, you know you need to purchase two 10-foot 2x12s for your side forms. **4**

Place one of the 2x12s on a pair of sawhorses, and lay out the treads, risers, and top step full-scale with a framing square. In the illustration, this layout is shown with dotted lines. Lay out these lines lightly; they won't be final cutting lines. For more on layout see "Lay Out the Stringers," page 122.

For drainage, the treads should slope downhill about ¼ inch per foot. The example steps have a run of 16 inches, so slope each tread about ⁵⁄₁₆ inch. Also, it's a good idea to slant the risers in about 1 inch to prevent stubbed toes. To make the slant adjustment, measure in 1 inch from the tread and riser intersections, as shown in the illustration. Then measure up ⁵⁄₁₆ inch for the slope adjustment. Use a circular saw to cut out the first form, then use the first form as a template to lay out the second form. Cut out the second form. **5**

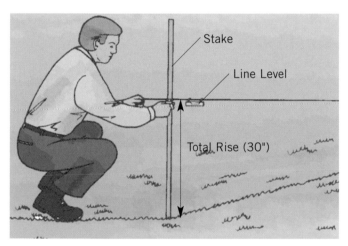

2 **Find the rise** by measuring up from the ground to the string on the downhill stake.

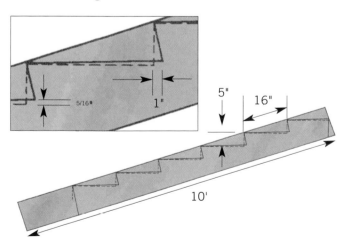

5 **For drainage purposes,** treads should slope downhill. Slant the bottom of the risers for safety.

(Continued on page 128)

EXCAVATE THE SITE

The concrete will need to be poured to a depth of 6 inches below grade. Excavate to that depth. You may need to excavate deep enough for a gravel base under the concrete—check your local codes. **6**

Set the side forms into the excavation. Make sure the forms are plumb at the top of the steps, as indicated in the illustration. Cut enough 24-inch-long 2x4 stakes to space them every 2 or 3 feet. Pound the stakes into the ground, and secure them to the form boards with 8d double-headed nails.

Cut two end form boards to 3 inches longer than the final step width. Nail one to each end of the side form boards.

Install the Riser Forms and Bracing. Rip two-by stock to equal the rise of the steps. For this example, rip 2x6s to 5 inches wide. When you make the rip cuts, set the blade of your saw to 45 degrees to create bevels. Place the bevel to the outside at the bottom, so you can reach the entire tread when you pour and finish the concrete. Cut the riser forms to the width of the final steps plus 3 inches for the width of the side forms.

Nail the riser forms across the side forms. To

Building Concrete Steps (Continued from page 127)

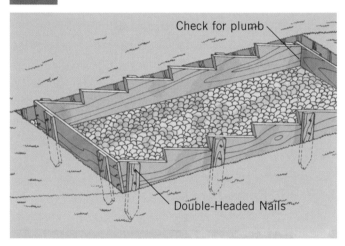

6 *Dig the trench. Support the forms using stakes fastened with double-headed nails.*

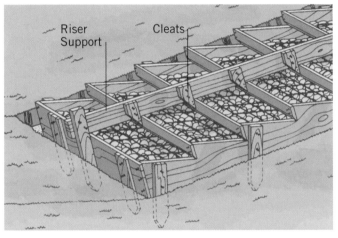

7 *Add a reinforcing mesh to the excavation. This will prevent the concrete from cracking.*

9 *Screed the concrete level with the top of the forms. Wide steps require a helper.*

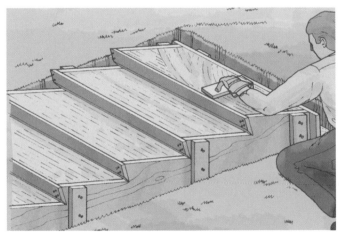

10 *Smooth the surface of the concrete using a darby. Make sweeping arcs with the tool.*

brace the form, lay a 2x6 up the stairs, centered side to side, as shown. Cut cleats with ends angled at 45 degrees. Place a cleat against each riser form, and nail it to the brace. Toenail the cleat to the risers. Toenail the brace to the uphill end of the form with no cleat. To keep concrete from sticking to the forms after you pour it, coat the forms with a release agent.

Place the Reinforcing Mesh. To provide added strength for your steps and prevent cracking, place wire mesh reinforcement in the form. **7** Reinforcing mesh must be completely embedded in the concrete. Use small stones, bricks, or pieces of broken concrete or concrete block to support the mesh so that it will be in the middle of the pour. Allow 2 inches between the edges of the mesh and the edges of the form. Overlap the pieces of mesh by 6 inches, and tie them together with wire.

Before you start mixing the concrete, spray the inside surfaces of the forms, the rubble fill if any, and the soil subgrade with water. This will keep them from drawing moisture from the concrete. Moistening the forms and soil is especially important on a warm, windy day.

Place the Concrete. Start dumping the concrete in the bottom step, making sure to fill the form completely. Fill the next step, using a shovel if you are transporting with a wheelbarrow. Tamp the concrete with a shovel to fill in corners and remove air voids. **8** Tap the outside of the form boards lightly with a hammer to settle the concrete around the perimeter of the forms.

As you place the concrete, lift up the wire reinforcing mesh with a hammer claw to make sure it is totally embedded.

Once you have filled the form with concrete, you can remove the middle brace. The danger of the forms bulging is greatest as the concrete is being flung down into the form. Begin to strike off, or screed, the surface of the concrete level with the top of the form. **9** Smooth the surface using a darby. **10** Use an edger to round the edges; use a wooden float to smooth the surface. **11** Remove the forms after one day. Keep the concrete moist for seven days to allow it to cure properly.

8 *Pour the concrete,* tamping it as you work to remove air pockets and ensure even coverage.

11 *Round off the edges* using a concrete edger; give a final smoothing with a wooden float.

smart tip

SLIP-RESISTANT STEPS
Make your steps safer by creating a slip-resistant finish. You can embed aggregate in the concrete, or brush the uncured surface with a broom. Below is a stamped concrete product.

Brick Steps

Mortared brick steps sit on a concrete base that keeps the bricks and joints from cracking as the ground moves with the weather. To build brick steps, follow the directions for building concrete steps, but add to your excavation depth the height of the bricks plus ½ inch for the mortar bed that holds the bricks on the concrete.

In laying out your steps, consider the size of the bricks so that each step will be made of whole units. The illustration below shows four different ways of creating brick risers and treads by using different brick thicknesses (1½ or 2¼

inches), laying the bricks flat, setting them on edge, and varying the mortar joint thickness (⅜ to ½ inch). These options give you some flexibility in achieving the exact riser height you need so that the risers add up to the correct overall height. The exposed length of the brick shown produces a tread of 12 inches.

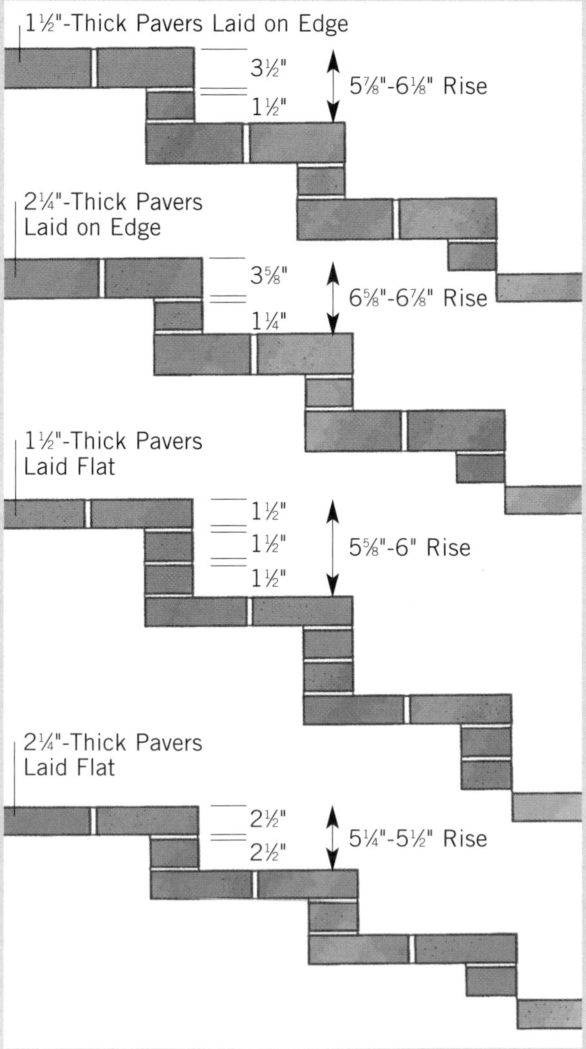

Tread Design. A tread width that is a multiple of 8 inches will accommodate the use of whole bricks. (Two 3⅝-inch-wide bricks laid flat plus two ⅜-inch mortar joints equals 8 inches.) If you draw a plan of the treads, you will be able to figure the number of paving bricks you'll need.

Once you've built the concrete base for the brick steps, the project is simply a matter of laying the bricks in the correct pattern and keeping the joints a consistent size.

BUILDING BRICK STEPS

To check the size of the base and the spacing of the pavers, lay out the units without mortar on at least two steps. Adjust the width of the mortar joints as necessary to get the best fit. **1**

The mortar bed holds the bricks in place and helps to compensate for minor irregularities in the concrete surface. Clean off the concrete surface, then start with the bottom step and mortar one tread at a time. Apply a bed of Type M or Type S ready-mix mortar. Make the mortar bed about ½ inch thick. Place the mortar, then smooth the surface with the flat side of a rectangular metal trowel; score the surface with a notched trowel.

Set the Brick. Spread mortar on the sides of the bricks with a trowel, and place them on the mortar setting bed, forming joints that are about ⅜ inch wide. **2** Cut off excess mortar with the edge of the trowel. Check the surface with a level, and tap the units gently with the trowel handle, if necessary, to bed them in the mortar.

The joints are ready for tooling when the mortar is "thumbprint" hard, meaning that you can press your thumb against the mortar and leave a print impression without the mortar sticking to your thumb. Using a rounded jointer, tool the short joints first, then the long joints to produce

No-Cut Step Patterns

1½"-Thick Pavers Laid on Edge

3½"
1½"
5⅞"-6⅛" Rise

2¼"-Thick Pavers Laid on Edge

3⅝"
1¼"
6⅝"-6⅞" Rise

1½"-Thick Pavers Laid Flat

1½"
1½"
1½"
5⅝"-6" Rise

2¼"-Thick Pavers Laid Flat

2½"
2½"
5¼"-5½" Rise

a concave-shaped joint. **3** Then finish the remaining steps. Mortar the next tread, and lay the brick as previously discussed until you finish the top step.

Clean the Steps. After the steps have set for about a week, brush the surface with a stiff natural- or synthetic-bristle brush—or a wire brush—to remove mortar drips and dust. Use a plastic or wooden scraper and a brush to remove large mortar splatters.

If necessary, clean the completed project with a diluted solution of muriatic acid (mixed 1:10 with water). Don't use muriatic acid on white,

cream, buff, gray, or brown brick, because it can leave ugly green or brown stains. Before applying an acidic cleaning solution, thoroughly wet the pavers with a garden hose. Wearing rubber gloves, apply the acid solution carefully with a special acid brush (made with polystyrene bristles, available from masonry suppliers). Scrub lightly; then rinse thoroughly with a garden hose. Be extremely careful when working with acid to avoid burns. Don't use metal tools or buckets because the acid will corrode them. Use plastic. To avoid dangerous splashes, always pour the water in the bucket first, then add the acid to the water.

Building Brick Steps on Concrete

TOOLS	MATERIALS
▨ Measuring tape	▨ Bricks or pavers
▨ Notched trowel	▨ Type M or Type S
▨ Pointed trowel	ready-mix mortar
▨ Rounded jointer	
▨ Muriatic acid	
▨ Rubber gloves	
▨ Garden hose	

1 *Lay a test run on the concrete base. Keep brick joints to a consistent size.*

2 *Spread mortar on the concrete and on the sides of the bricks—also called "buttering."*

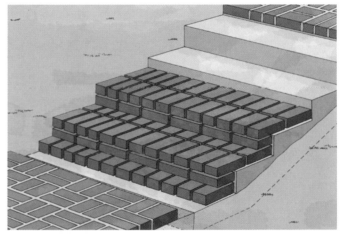

3 *Tool the joints when the mortar is thumbprint hard to produce a concave joint.*

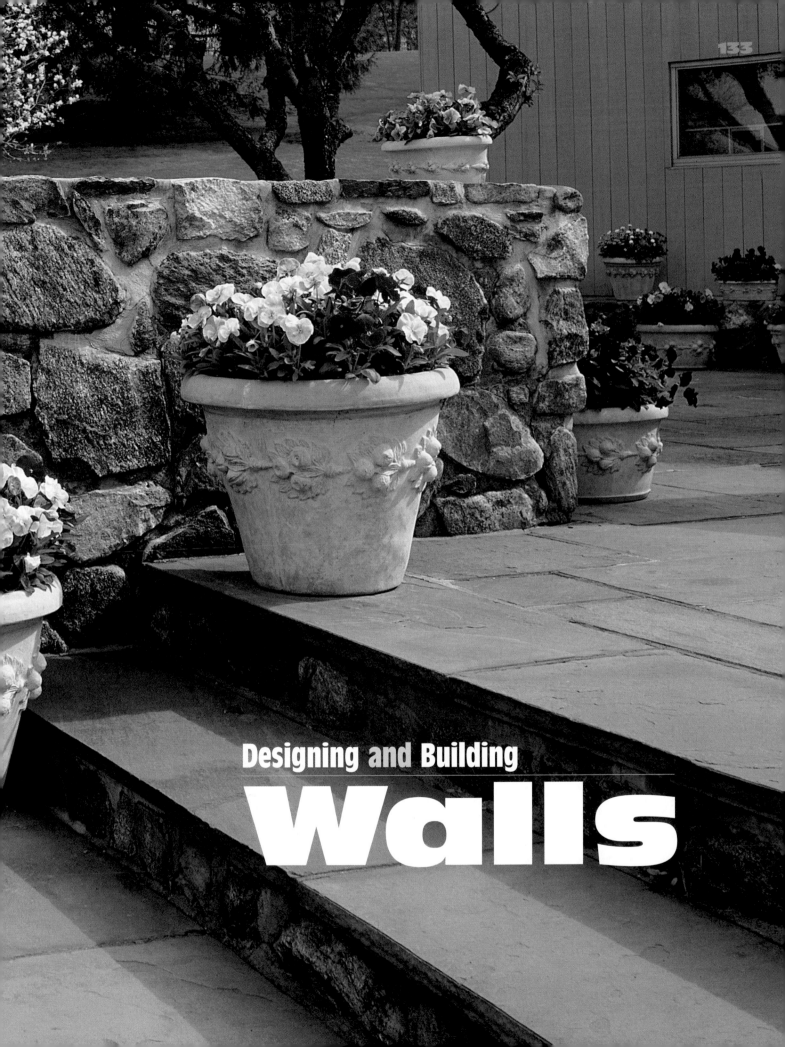

Designing and Building
Walls

1

2

1 To soften the look of tall privacy walls, place boxes of plants at the top or add climbing vines and trellises.

2 Using stones of different sizes and shapes lends a naturalistic look to dry-laid stone walls.

3

4

Gallery of Wall Designs

5

3 Part of the appeal of stone walls is how effortlessly they seem to blend in with the surrounding area.

4 Give a stone wall for your yard a natural appearance by using stones that are indigenous to the area.

5 Using brick offers the opportunity for adding custom features, such as this fountain niche.

6 A low stone wall topped by a white picket fence adds a distinctive design touch to the front of this house.

6

Gallery of Wall Designs

1 Add a dash of color to your yardscape by adding a colorizing agent to the stucco mixture.

2 Landscape walls can be barriers or dividers, and they can also add a decorative element.

3 This low wall is made of interlocking blocks, an easy-to-build wall system.

4 Stone walls are durable. A dry-laid wall like this one does not require a concrete footing.

5 Stucco-covered block walls make good privacy barriers; they also provide a good backdrop for plantings and general garden design.

6 Tame steeply-sloping yards by adding retaining walls that create a stepped series of level terraces.

7 Rather than play it straight, the designer of this wall added a distinctive curve to the design.

8 Picturesque is how many people describe stone walls. Even one in need of some maintenance has a certain charm.

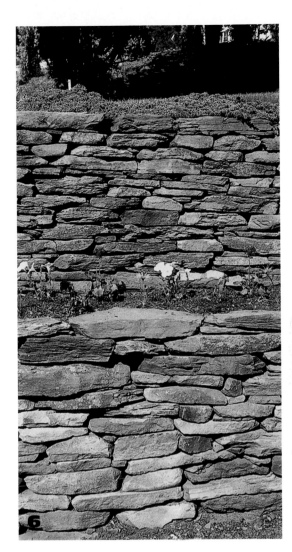

CHAPTER 8

Dry-Laid Stone Walls

Tools

Types of Stone

Wall Building Basics

Constructing the Wall

Stonework is one of the few crafts that requires little more than a strong back and some patience. Most of it doesn't require specialized skills or tools; it's just plain hard work. As long as you are prepared for the physical work and the mental challenge of putting together what is, in effect, a three-dimensional jigsaw puzzle in stone, building a stone wall can be enjoyable.

A dry-laid stone wall is the simplest of masonry jobs. No footing is required (as long as the wall is less than 3 feet high). There is no mortar to mix and no joints to fuss over. Walls laid 100 years ago are still standing in excellent shape, so a dry-laid wall can be a beautiful and permanent part of your landscape.

Tools

The tools you'll need for a dry-laid wall are elementary. Get a tape measure, a sharp-bladed shovel, a pickax for removing stones in the way of the wall, and a stonemason's hammer and chisel. Stakes, string, a mason's level, and a site-made batter gauge will aid in laying out and stacking the wall.

A prybar comes in handy for moving stones. Wear heavy leather gloves for handling stones and safety glasses when splitting them. Stone walls more than 3 feet high may require special construction techniques and are best left to an experienced stonemason.

RUBBLE AND FIELDSTONE

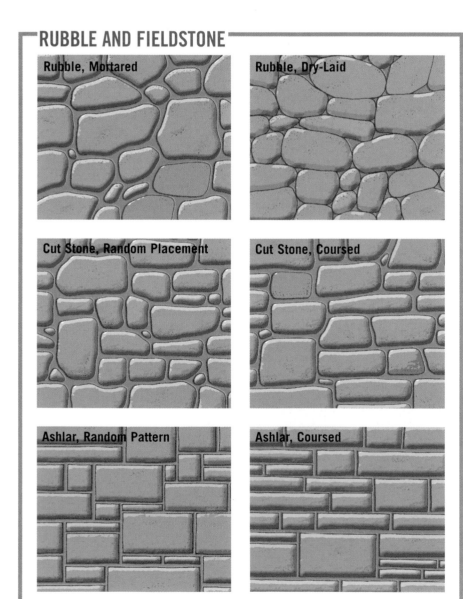

Rubble, Mortared

Rubble, Dry-Laid

Cut Stone, Random Placement

Cut Stone, Coursed

Ashlar, Random Pattern

Ashlar, Coursed

Types of Stones

Stones used for wall construction can be divided into two broad categories: cut stone and rubble. Generally, the exact kinds of stone are limited to the types found in your area. Stones sold at masonry and patio supply houses and at stone yards can be expensive. You may save money by finding stones elsewhere. Stones from road-construction sites, local farmers, building-demolition sites, and landscape-remodeling projects may be free for the hauling. Also check the classified section of the newspaper.

If you decide to scrounge your own stones, you'll need a sturdy pickup truck or a trailer with good springs and tires to haul the rock away. It doesn't take many stones to add up to a ton, so you may find yourself making more trips than anticipated. When budgeting, factor in your time, gasoline, and wear-and-tear on the vehicle.

Rubble and Fieldstone. Rubble consists of irregularly shaped stones. The stones are often those blasted or bulldozed from road construction sites or pieces left over from cutting trimmed stones at the quarry. Rubble is usually the least expensive stone you can buy.

Fieldstones generally have rounded edges as a result of glacial or water action. As the name implies, some of these stones are taken from plowed fields. Others are from along a creek or river.

Cut Stone. Cut stone, also referred to as quarried stone, is available semidressed or fully dressed from stone yards and landscape suppliers. Semidressed stones, such as cobblestones, are roughly square with smooth sides and uniform thickness. Fully dressed stones, called ashlar, are trimmed to more precise rectangular shapes.

SELECTING STONES

Whether you buy them or scrounge them, choose stones with flat sides and edges. This is especially important if you're building a dry-laid wall, because the only thing holding the stone in place is its weight. Select stones with at least three flat sides: the top, bottom, and the side to be used for the face of the wall. Avoid large egg-shaped or round stones, but make sure you have a good variety of sizes and shapes to provide the best design and construction.

Walls look best if they contain a good mixture of large and small stones of different colors, set randomly over the entire surface. Set small

Above Found stones can make good walls, but dressed quarry stones offer a neater, more professional-looking appearance, even in dry-laid walls.

stones around large ones. Avoid grouping too many stones of one size or color in one area of the wall.

Although the project will go faster if you use large stones, make sure that they move easily and aren't too large or heavy to lift. Generally, stones that weigh from 15 to 30 pounds are easy to work with and will be in scale with most backyard garden projects.

smart tip

MAKE A BATTER GAUGE
Stone walls should slope inward from bottom to top. To check inward slope, use a batter, or slope gauge, with a level. Make the gauge from 1x2s joined at one end and spread apart at the other. The difference between the two ends is the slope you want to maintain. The level should read plumb when held against the wall.

Build the gauge using 1x2s with a spread equal to the wall's slope.

The level reads plumb when the slope gauge rests against the wall.

Above Dry-laid stone walls have a natural appearance that seems to blend in with the surrounding area.

ESTIMATING AMOUNTS

Stone is sold by the cubic yard or by the ton. To estimate the cubic yards of stone you'll need, multiply wall width by length by height—all measured in feet. Divide this number by 27. It's a good idea to order an extra 10 percent to compensate for breakage. If the stone is sold by the ton, have the stone dealer determine the number of tons needed for your wall project.

If you're scrounging your own rubble or fieldstone, simply measure the volume of each truckload, then divide this figure into the volume of the wall to determine the number of loads needed. Allow 25 percent extra to compensate for voids between the stones when they are tossed randomly in the truck.

When you get the stones home, sort them by size into different groups near the construction site. First find flat stones wide enough to span the full thickness of the wall. You'll put these stones every 4 to 6 feet in the wall to tie together the two parallel rows that make up the front and back of the wall. Place these stones, called bond stones, near where they will be laid. Then find other stones with straight edges and sides. Place them at the ends, or corners, of the wall. Place them near where they will be laid, too. It's best to spread the end and bond stones in groups one layer thick about 4 to 6

feet away from the proposed base so that you can spot the stone you need.

Wall Building Basics

Dry-laid stone walls lend a rustic appearance to the landscape, and they are easy to build once you develop an eye for picking the right stones and fitting them together. A dry-laid stone wall makes a good low retaining wall: the spaces between the stones prevent water from building up behind the wall, as can sometimes happen with a mortared wall.

BUILDING REQUIREMENTS

A freestanding dry-laid wall can be straight or can have corners, curves, or any combination of these. Because the wall is held together by nothing more than gravity, your main goal is to avoid building a wall that is top heavy.

A rule of thumb is that a wall up to 3 feet high must be at least 2 feet wide. Freestanding walls more than 2 feet high generally have a slight inward slope, or batter, from the bottom to the top. Battered wall faces lean against each other, holding the stones in place. Walls up to 3 feet high should have 1 inch of batter for each 2 feet of rise, though a wall 2 feet or less can be built with a plumb face.

Footings. Dry-laid walls less than 3 feet high usually require no footings. If the soil is firm, you can lay the stones directly on the ground. For best appearance and stability, lay the first course of stones below grade.

Bond Patterns. Freestanding stone walls are typically stacked two stones thick; these parallel face courses are called wythes. To tie the wythes together, bond stones are placed at each end of the wall and at 4- to 6-foot intervals in each course of the wall. Usually, the more bond stones you can incorporate into the wall, the stronger it will be. As you build each successive course, stagger the joints between stones so that each stone rests on at least two stones beneath it. Gaps can be filled with small rubble stones.

Constructing the Wall

The work will go easier if you sort the stones you need to build the wall—bond stones, end stones, cap stones—and spread them along the wall location. **1** Have a helper or two on hand to lend a hand when lifting heavy stones into position.

After deciding on the location and the length of the wall, drive temporary stakes into the ground to mark the ends of the wall. Stretch mason's line between the stakes to mark the sides of the wall. You can also place a line level on the string and use it as a guide to keeping the wall level. Dig a trench between the lines. Remove any sod or loose topsoil with a flat-bladed shovel. Dig the actual trench with a pointed shovel. Dig the trench so that at least half of—but preferably the entire—first course will be below grade. Provide as smooth an area as possible for the first course. **2**

THE FIRST COURSE

Select large, relatively flat stones for the base, but save the flattest stones for capping the wall, as described later. Start by placing large bond stones at each end of the wall, with the flattest side up. **3** Dig out the ground, if necessary, so

Constructing the Wall

TOOLS	MATERIALS
◼ Work gloves	◼ Stones
◼ Mason's trowel	◼ Shims or wedges
◼ Shovel	◼ Mortar mix
◼ Spirit Level	◼ Cap stones
◼ Hawk	◼ Stakes and string
◼ Mortar Box	
◼ Hammer	
◼ Batter gauge (optional)	

1 *Group the stones* before you start building. Use the flattest stones for the first course.

2 *Dig into the soil* to provide a smooth, flat base for the first course of stones.

3 *Use a flat, double-width stone* at the head of both rows at the ends of the wall.

(Continued on page 144)

that the stones sit firmly in the trench without rocking.

You'll find it easier to lay the front and back of the wall simultaneously. Lay two parallel wythes so that the outside of each stone is directly below the string. Place bond stones every 4 to 6 feet. Measure down from the string as you work to make sure the course is level. The base stones can lean slightly toward the center of the wall. **4** This helps create wall sides that lean against each other for stability. Fill the void in the center of the wall with small stones. **5** Continue in this manner as you work your way down the length of the wall.

THE SECOND COURSE

Move your strings so that they're about 3 inches above the top of the second course. If the wall has a batter, place the top outside edge of the stones slightly inside the string. Stagger the joints along the faces and along the ends of the wall as well. Place one stone over two, and two stones over one. **6** Set the front and back wythes simultaneously, filling in the gaps with small stones as you go. **7** Check frequently with your level or batter gauge. **8**

If a stone teeters on a point or sharp corner, you may be able to chisel off the projection to make the stone sit firmly. In some cases, you

Constructing the Wall *(Continued from page 143)*

4 *Lay the stones* to a guide along the outside edge of the wall. Face irregular edges inward.

5 *Fill interior gaps* between larger stones with smaller stones and rubble.

8 *Dry-laid stone walls* should slope inward slightly. Use a level or batter gauge to check your work.

9 *As you work,* prop up larger stones by using small stones as wedges.

can place small wedge-shaped stones between larger ones to hold them in position and prevent rocking. **9** If possible, place these small wedges toward the inside of the wall where they won't be knocked out of place.

Continue laying up courses in the same manner, maintaining the correct batter angle as you go. Ideally, bond stones should be placed in each course every 4 to 6 feet and staggered so that they don't fall in line with the bond stones underneath. If you don't have enough large stones to span both wythes, place bond stones in every other course. As you build the wall, use the squarest stones at the ends. If the wall turns a corner, use overlapping bond stones to link the two meeting walls at the intersection.

CAP THE WALL

Use the flattest, broadest, and best-looking stones for the top course, or cap. Because cap stones are often easily knocked off low walls, you may want to mortar the cap in place. If so, spread a 2-inch-thick layer of mortar over the top course. **10** Embed the cap stones in the mortar. **11** An alternative to cap stones is to finish off the top with a solid mortar cap. The cap should be 2 to 4 inches thick and crowned slightly to facilitate water runoff.

6 *Span the width of the wall* using a double-wide stone. This helps tie the wall together.

7 *In alternative courses* at the ends of the wall, install square-edged cross stones.

10 *Trowel mortar* over the top courses to level the area and to form a base for the cap stones.

11 *Press the cap stones* into place. Cut stones so that they overhang the wall slightly.

8

Dry-Laid Stone Walls

CHAPTER 9

Footings for Walls

General Requirements

Buying Concrete

Mixing Concrete

Building Footings

Pouring Concrete

A mortared wall is rigid. Unfortunately, the ground below it isn't. As a result, mortared walls should have a strip of concrete, called a footing, beneath them. Without a footing, a wall is at the mercy of the soil, which may not offer enough support or stability to keep the wall from sinking, cracking, or collapsing. A concrete footing spreads the weight of the wall over the soil, bridges soft spots that can cause walls to crack, and provides support as the soil settles or moves.

General Requirements

The size of the footing and the way you construct it depends on the climate, soil conditions, and the height and weight of the wall it must support. Building codes are very specific on footing requirements, so be sure to check with your local building department.

FOOTING SIZE AND DEPTH

As a rule of thumb, footing width should be either twice that of the wall, or two-thirds the wall height, whichever is greater. If you plan to build a brick wall that incorporates pilasters into the design, make sure the footing follows the shape of the wall, or make the footing wide enough to accommodate the extra width of the pilasters. As with all masonry walls, the top of the footing should be several inches below ground level so that it won't show once the wall is built.

Footings should be at least 6 inches thick. If frost heave is a problem, the footing should be set below the frost line. Codes vary as to the exact depth, so check with your building department for standards in your area.

Poor Drainage. In soil with poor drainage (regardless of frost-line depth), place the footing on a tamped gravel base at least 6 inches thick. The gravel base prevents water from accumulating beneath the footing, keeping soil movement to a minimum. If you are unsure of the drainage in your area, ask local building officials about the types of wall footings they recommend for your project.

FOOTING FORMS

Forms, usually two-by boards, hold wet concrete to the shape required for the footing. In firm soil that retains its shape after digging, the excavation itself can be the form. In this case, place leveled 2x4s at the top of the excavation. You'll need the 2x4s as a guide when you level the concrete. For loose soil, use wide boards (2x6s, 2x8s, 2x10s, etc.) that extend the full depth of the footing. Once the concrete hardens, the forms are usually removed. (See "Footings and Forms," opposite.)

Buying Concrete

Concrete consists of a mixture of Portland cement, sand, and gravel. Depending on the size of the job and your budget, you can buy bags of premixed concrete and add water; you can buy the ingredients and mix your own; or you can have a wet-concrete mix delivered by truck.

DRY MIXES

Purchasing dry concrete mix in 60- or 80-pound bags may prove convenient for jobs requiring less than ½ cubic yard of concrete. But because it takes about twenty 80-pound sacks to make a ½ cubic yard, larger jobs can be quite expensive and labor intensive. If you use premixed bags, it may be worthwhile to have them delivered. Make sure none of the sacks has already hardened. Be sure to store the concrete somewhere dry and off the ground on something like a pallet.

Mixing Your Own. You can usually save money on jobs requiring more than ½ cubic yard of concrete by buying cement and aggregates separately and mixing them yourself. Cement is sold by the 94-pound sack. (Type I cement is commonly used in residential work. Types II through IV are used in more massive structures.) Masons refer to sand as fine aggregate and gravel as coarse aggregate. Both are sold by the cubic yard. For home use, cement is commonly mixed with bank-run sand, because the round particles make for a stronger mix. For coarse aggregate, use stone or gravel ranging from ½ to 1½ inches in diameter.

All aggregates must be free of silt and debris. To test, place about 2 inches of aggregate in a glass jar. Pour in water, and shake gently. Wait for the water to clear. If there is more than ⅛ inch of silt on top of the aggregate, you'll have to wash it. Simply dump the aggregate on a clean, hard surface, and hose it down.

WET MIXES

For concrete footings and walls requiring 1 or more cubic yards of concrete, ordering a wet, or transit mix, may be your best bet. The wet concrete can be poured directly into the footings from the truck, saving hours of back-breaking labor. If the truck can't get to within about 20 feet of the forms, the concrete can be pumped from the truck through a hose. This method usually costs extra. A cheaper but more difficult method is to cart the concrete to the forms with a few wheelbarrows and some strong backs.

Air-Entrained Concrete. In cold climates subject to severe freeze/thaw conditions, air-entrained concrete is common. This type of concrete contains millions of tiny air pockets that allow water to freeze and expand without damaging the concrete. The air-entraining agent can be added to Types I, II, and III concrete, but you'll need a power mixer to activate the agent in the mix. Check with your concrete supplier to find out if air-entrained concrete is common in your area.

ESTIMATING AMOUNTS

The amount of concrete required for a footing is the biggest determining factor when deciding how to order concrete. To figure out the amount needed, multiply the footing width by its depth, working in inches. Divide by 144 to get square feet. Then multiply this figure by the overall length of the footing in feet to get cubic feet. To figure cubic yards, divide the number of cubic feet by 27.

The easiest way to determine quantities is to provide a concrete supplier with the footing dimensions and let them compute the amounts of each ingredient and an overall price.

FOOTINGS AND FORMS

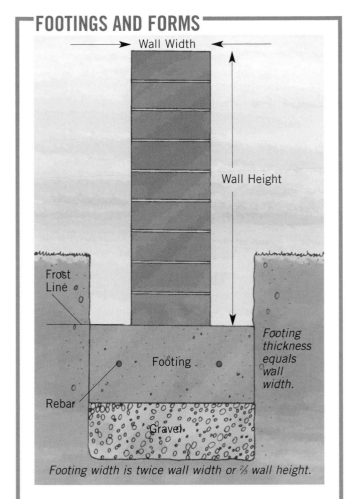

Footing width is twice wall width or ⅔ wall height.

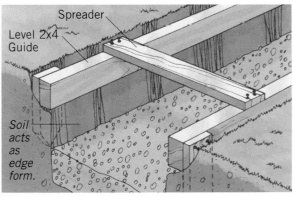

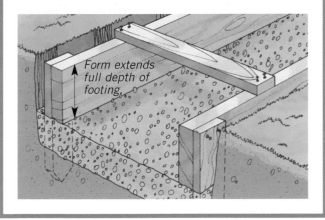

Mixing Concrete

Whether you're using a premix or separate ingredients, decide if you want to mix the concrete by hand or rent a power mixer. Weigh the rental costs against the time and effort you'll save by using a power mixer. A power mixer also ensures a more even mix and is a necessity when mixing air-entrained concrete.

MIXING BY HAND

Hand mixing concrete involves a square-point shovel or a mason's hoe to combine concrete ingredients. Hand mixing is hard work. While you can mix the ingredients in a wheelbarrow, it's usually easier to mix them on a clean, flat surface, such as an old sheet of plywood, or in a mortar box (also called a concrete barge).

Measure the Ingredients. The table "Concrete Ingredients by Proportion," page 152, shows the proportions of cement, sand, aggregate, and water needed to make concrete. Use 1½-inch aggregate for concrete used in footings. For mixing purposes, you can measure proportions by the bucket or shovel or with a measuring box like the one shown. **1** A measuring box is built to measure exactly 1 cubic foot of dry ingredients. Make the box from lumber or plywood so the inside dimensions are 12 x 12 x 12 inches.

Use the same amount of ingredients for each batch. Place the materials in layers on top of one another. Begin with the gravel; then add sand and then cement.

Mix the Dry Ingredients. If you're working on a flat surface or mixing the ingredients in a wheelbarrow, use a mason's hoe or rake to mix the dry ingredients thoroughly before adding the water. **2**

Add Water. The water should be dirt free—clean enough to drink. The exact amount of water varies, in part because of the moisture content of the aggregate. To determine the amount of water generally required in a mix, check the table "Concrete Ingredients by Proportion," page 152. As a rule of thumb, add 6 to 7 gallons of water for every 90-pound bag of cement in the mix. If you use too little water, the concrete won't be fluid enough to fill out the form. Too much water results in weak concrete. Start with 1 or 2 gallons of water, and keep track of the amount you use so that you can add the same amount to subsequent batches.

smart tip

RECIPE FOR FOOTINGS
A mix of 1 part cement, 3 parts sand, and 5 parts gravel (called a 1:3:5 mix) is typical for footings. Ask your local masonry supplier to recommend an appropriate mix for your situation.

Mixing Concrete

TOOLS

- Wheelbarrow
- Work gloves
- Rake
- Shovel
- Hoe
- Bucket

MATERIALS

- Plywood for measuring box
- Plywood for mixing surface
- Gravel
- Sand
- Cement

1 **Construct a plywood** box measuring 12 x 12 x 12 in. to measure out the dry ingredients.

Make sure to mix all ingredients thoroughly, scraping any unmixed cement and aggregate from the sides and bottom of the box or pile. The concrete mix should be an even color and the same consistency throughout.

If mixing on a flat surface, make a shallow depression in the center of the dry mix with your hoe, then pour in a little water. **3** Mix thoroughly by pulling dry material from the edges into the depression. If using a mortar box, place the dry materials so that they fill about two-thirds of the box, leaving an empty space in the box on the side nearest the forms. Add water to the empty end, then pull the dry materials into the water, mixing them together as you go. Continue adding water in small amounts while turning over the mix.

Test the Mix. You can tell if the concrete has too little or too much water by using the blade of your hoe or shovel to make ridges in it. (See the Smart Tip on page 155.) If the mix is too wet, it usually doesn't have enough sand and coarse aggregate for the amount of cement. Add 5 to 10 percent more aggregate; mix well; and retest. Keep careful notes of the added amounts.

USING A POWER MIXER

Power mixers come in two varieties: electrically powered and gas powered. If you rent a gas-powered mixer, have the rental people start the engine to make sure it operates easily. If you use an electric mixer, make sure you can provide electricity to the mixing site. If an extension cord is required, check that the wire gauge is heavy enough to handle the amperage drawn by the motor. If the cord is long, use a wire gauge that is even heavier than required: the available voltage drops as electricity travels along a wire. The rental people can advise you on the appropriate type of cord for the job. Position the mixer as close to the sand and gravel piles as possible.

With the mixer turned off, add the amounts of dry ingredients needed. Measure carefully, and keep track of the amounts so that subsequent batches are consistent. You may need to experiment with different proportions at first. Turn on the mixer, and run it for a few minutes to allow the dry ingredients to mix thoroughly. With the mixer running, pour in a small amount of water, and allow it to mix in. Continue adding water a little at a time until the mixture reaches the correct consistency. If you're not familiar with this method, it's a good idea to stop the mixer periodically and check the mix, as described above. Once the concrete is mixed, tilt the mixer barrel to pour the concrete into a wheelbarrow for transport to the forms. Have a helper hold the wheelbarrow steady.

9

Footings for Walks

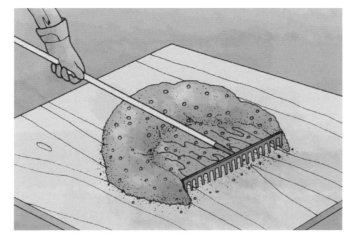

2 *Mix the dry ingredients* thoroughly before adding water. A rake or hoe works best.

3 *Add water,* and mix the ingredients together, scrapping up loose material as you go.

Building Footings

Once you've established where to build a wall, use stakes, string, and batter boards to mark the footing location and to guide in digging trenches and positioning forms. If your wall will define property lines, be sure the footing is properly positioned so that you don't have to tear down the wall later.

Layout of Footings. For a straight wall, drive stakes into the ground to mark the four corners. For a wall that turns a corner, drive a stake at each end of the wall and one at the outside corner of the wall.

Measure out 3 to 4 feet beyond each stake, and erect a set of batter boards. The horizontal boards should be at least 1 foot wider than the anticipated width of the footing trench. Align the center of the board with the rough center point of the proposed wall.

On the crosspieces, measure the wall width from the string and mark the other face of the wall (labeled A in "Batter Board Layout," opposite top right). Measure to find the inside and outside faces of the footing (B) and the outside edges of the footing trench (C); mark them on the board, too. Remember that the footing width is either twice as wide as the wall or two-thirds the wall height, whichever is greater. The trench itself should be 1 or 2 feet wider than the footing to provide room for installing the formwork. At each mark, use a handsaw to make shallow cuts in the crosspieces to hold the strings in place.

BUILDING FORMS

After you dig the trench, compact the soil in the trench bottom with a hand tamper to prevent settling. Then fill the entire trench bottom with at least 6 inches of gravel.

Install the Stakes. Drive 2x4 stakes at the outside corners of the trench. Stretch string between the corner stakes, and level it with the help of a string level. Use the string as a guide to install intermediate stakes about every 2 feet. If the form boards are long enough to reach between the corner stakes, you may find it easier to attach and level the form boards first, then use them as a guide to install the intermediate stakes.

If form boards are not long enough, create a butt joint between the boards, and secure it with a plywood gusset. **1**

Attach the form boards by driving nails or screws through the stakes into the boards. Double-check the form boards frequently with a 4-foot level to make sure they remain level.

Brace the Formwork. If the form boards are 2x6s or wider, install 1x4 stretchers across the board tops at 4- to 6-foot intervals to keep the concrete from spreading the forms. **2**

Place rebar between the forms, according to local building codes. Rebar should be about one-third of the way up from the bottom of the footing. For shallow footings, prop the rebar above the trench bottom on bricks. **3** Keep the bars at least 1 inch away from the form boards.

CONCRETE INGREDIENTS BY PROPORTION

Maximun Size Coarse Aggregate	Air-Entrained Concrete Number of Parts per Ingredient				Concrete without Air Number of Parts per Ingredient			
	Cement	Sand*	Coarse Aggregate	Water	Cement	Sand*	Coarse Aggregate	Water
⅜	1	2¼	1½	½	1	2½	1½	½
½	1	2¼	2	½	1	2½	2	½
¾	1	2¼	2½	½	1	2½	2½	½
1	1	2¼	2¾	½	1	2½	2¾	½
1½	1	2¼	3	½	1	2½	3	½

Note: 7.48 gallons of water equals 1 cubic foot. One 94-lb.bag of portland cement equals about 1 cubic foot.
* "wet" sand sold for most construction use.
The combined finished volume is approximately two-thirds the sum of the original bulk volumes.

Using the 3-4-5 Method

Here's a method that ensures corners are square. Mark one string tied to a batter board 3 feet from the corner. Mark the other string 4 feet from the corner. Measure the distance between the marks. If it is 5 feet, the corner is square. If it isn't, adjust the string until the distance is correct.

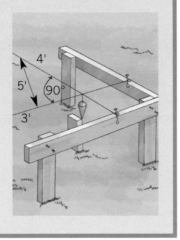

BATTER BOARD LAYOUT

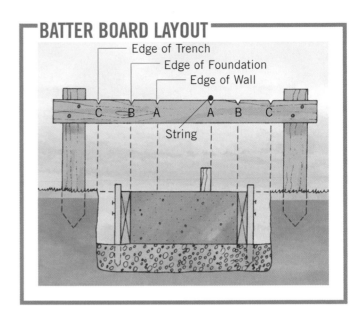

Edge of Trench
Edge of Foundation
Edge of Wall

C B A A B C

String

Building Forms

TOOLS

- Shovels
- Measuring tape
- Work gloves
- Tampers
- Wheelbarrows
- Drill-driver
- Screws
- Level

MATERIALS

- Lumber for forms
- Gravel
- Rebar
- Wire for rebar

1 *Secure forms to stakes.* *Where form boards meet, construct a plywood gusset.*

2 *For large forms, install stretchers every 4 to 6 feet to prevent the boards from spreading.*

3 *Prop rebar on bricks or some other material. Secure rebar with metal wire.*

9

Footings for Walks

Above *Tall mortared walls require strong footings to compensate for the natural movement of the earth.*

Pouring Concrete

After the formwork is complete, prepare the site for pouring concrete. Clean up anything that will be in the way. Make sure you can get the concrete to the forms. Brush some clean motor oil or form-release agent onto the inside of the form boards so that the concrete won't bond to them. Sprinkle the trench with water. The gravel should be moist so that it won't suck water from the concrete, but do not allow puddles to form.

Pour the Concrete. Starting at one end of the form, pour the concrete. Have several helpers with shovels available to spread the concrete in the forms as it is poured. **1** Do not allow the concrete to mound up in one area. If you are pouring wet-mix concrete, move the chute along the form, placing the concrete in an even layer. Use a shovel to spread the concrete evenly in the form and to tamp it in place. Work the shovel with a slicing motion to eliminate any voids or air pockets in the concrete. **2** Work the concrete into corners. **3**

Screed the Forms. Pull a scrap piece of 2x4 along the tops of the forms to level off, or screed, the concrete. **4** Work in a zigzag motion from one end of the form to the other. The purpose of screeding is to knock down any high spots and fill in any voids. The surface can be left slightly rough to provide good "tooth" for

the mortar bed on which you'll set the masonry units for the wall. If you plan to build a double-thickness brick wall or hollow concrete-block retaining wall, vertical rebar may be required. Place the rebar in the footing while the concrete is still wet. **5**

Allow the concrete to cure for about one week before building the wall. During this time, keep the concrete moist by sprinkling it with water several times a day, then covering it with plastic sheeting. When curing is complete, remove the forms. Carefully pull out the nails or screws securing the form boards to the stakes, and gently pry the form boards away from the footing.

 Pouring

TOOLS	MATERIALS
▨ **Work gloves**	▨ **Concrete**
▨ **Shovels**	▨ **Rebar**
▨ **Landscape sheeting**	
▨ **Screed**	
▨ **Trowels**	
▨ **Prybar**	

3 **Work the concrete** *into corners and against the form boards using a trowel.*

TELLING WHEN CONCRETE IS READY

After mixing, test the consistency of the concrete by placing a good-size clump on a clean surface. Work the mixture briefly with a trowel. If the mixture is too wet, ridges made with the trowel won't hold their shape. If the mixture is too dry, you won't be able to make ridges at all as the concrete will form dry lumps (right). When the mixture is ready, the concrete will hold most of its shape and only a little water will be visible (far right).

1 *Spread out the concrete* as it is poured into the forms. Try to pour the concrete in an even layer.

2 *Using a shovel,* slice into the concrete to remove air pockets and distribute the mixture.

4 *Screed the poured concrete* by running a 2x4 in a back-and-forth motion over the forms.

5 *Install rebar* while the concrete is still wet. Concrete takes about one week to cure fully.

CHAPTER 10

Mortared Stone Walls

General Requirements for Stone Walls

Constructing the Wall

Building a mortared stone wall requires more time and effort than constructing a dry-laid wall, but the mortared wall is sturdier and has a more formal, solid appearance. Mortared walls generally require less maintenance than dry-laid walls. Because the wall will have a foundation, check with your local building department to find out whether you need a building permit.

General Requirements for Stone Walls

Fitting the stones in a mortared wall is not as demanding as it is for a dry-laid wall—the mortar fills in gaps. For this reason, a mortared wall is a good option when you have a limited selection of stone shapes and sizes. It's the only option when you're working with river or creek stones: round creekbed stones won't work in a dry-laid wall.

Mortar allows you to set irregularly shaped or rounded stones firmly, with the best faces exposed. Unlike dry-laid walls, which must slope inward as they go up, stone walls 3 feet and under are built with plumb sides. For a strong wall, however, it is good practice to use bond stones and to stagger the joints.

Footings. Mortared stone walls are inflexible, and they require concrete footings as a result. For walls less than 2 feet high, the footing may be as simple as a shallow trench dug to the width of the wall and filled with several inches of concrete. For higher, wider walls, the footing should be twice the width of the wall. The footing should be as thick as the wall is wide. In cold climates, the footing should extend below the frost line. For some areas that would be 36 inches below the surface. Check with your building department to see what local code requires. The top of the footing should be several inches below ground level so that it won't show once you build the wall. For complete instructions on installing wall footings, see Chapter 9, "Wall Footings," page 146. Allow the footing to cure for at least three days before building the wall.

Mortar. The mortar mix used for stone walls is called a Type N mix. It consists of 1 part portland cement, 1 part lime, and 6 parts sand, all mixed with about 5 parts water. For small projects, it's usually best to buy premixed mortar in sacks; you just add the water. For larger projects, you can save money by buying the dry ingredients separately and making your own mortar mix. Some masons prefer to substitute fireclay for lime in the mix to make it more workable. Mixes containing lime can stain the stones, so if you use a lime mix, test it on your stones. Add water sparingly to make a dry, stiff mix that supports the stones and won't squeeze out of the joints. The best way to compute the amount of mortar needed is to build a short section of mortared wall (say, 3 feet tall by 5 feet long) and note the amount of mortar required. Multiply this amount by the number of 5-foot sections in the wall to figure the amount needed for the rest of the wall. Rubble and fieldstone walls will require more mortar than walls constructed of neatly fitting cut stones or ashlar.

Tools. You will need tools for mixing and applying concrete and mortar, including a shovel, wheelbarrow, mason's trowel, and measuring tape. You'll also need a sharp-bladed shovel and a pickax for removing stones in the way of the wall. Stakes, string, and a mason's level help in laying out and stacking the wall. A pry bar comes in handy for moving stones.

MORTARED STONE WALL

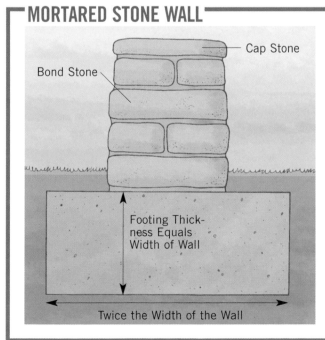

Cap Stone

Bond Stone

Footing Thickness Equals Width of Wall

Twice the Width of the Wall

Above *The arrangement of stones looks random, but notice how the mason staggered the joints between courses to ensure a long-lasting wall.*

Below *Retaining walls like this one do a good job of holding back the hillside. Provide weep holes near the bottom of the wall for proper drainage.*

Constructing the Wall

Mortared stone walls are built much like dry-laid walls, although the work will progress considerably more slowly. Select bond stones, end stones, and cap stones, and spread them along the course of the wall. Select the remaining stones one course at a time, and test-fit them without mortar first.

Make a Trial Run. About one week after pouring the footing (it will take at least that long to cure), mark the wall's sides and ends on it with a chalk line. Place the end stones, and set bond stones every 4 to 6 feet along the foundation. Fit the remaining stones so that joints between them are narrow but no less than about ½ inch wide. Fill voids between large stones with smaller ones. Arrange the stones with the flattest, broadest sides facing down to ensure a good mortar bond to the footing. **1**

Once you're satisfied with the fit, remove the stones and lay them in order on their respective sides of the footing. Make sure the stones are clean and dry before you set them permanently.

Lay the First Course. Starting at an end, spread a 2-inch-thick layer of mortar about 3 feet long between the chalk lines on the footing. **2** Carefully set the end stones, and tap them lightly with a mallet or hammer until they are approximately level. Then lay stones next to the end stone to start the wythes that will be the front and back of the wall.

Mortar between the Stones. Once you've laid enough stones to cover the mortar bed, use a pointed trowel to mortar all the joints between the stones. **3** Pick up a glob of mortar on the trowel; hold the trowel several inches above the joint and parallel with it; and using a downward flip, fling the mortar into the joint. Generally, the mortar will settle by itself to fill in any voids; you needn't tamp it in. Remove excess or squeezed-out mortar from joints with your trowel. If some mortar gets on the stone face, immediately wipe away the mortar using a damp sponge.

Guide the Courses. Although the stones will vary in height, try to keep the course level. Set up stakes and level strings so that they are about 3 inches above the top outside edges of the first course. **4** Measure down from the strings, making sure both ends of the stones are the same distance from the string. If a stone is too low, raise it by placing more mortar underneath it. If it's too high, push down on it to squeeze out more mortar.

Build End and Corner Leads. Once you've laid the first course, you build up the ends and corners before filling in the rest of the other

Constructing

TOOLS	MATERIALS
◼ **Chalk-line box**	◼ **Lumber for forms**
◼ **Shovels**	◼ **Gravel**
◼ **Measuring tape**	◼ **Form release agent**
◼ **Work gloves**	◼ **Stones**
◼ **Rakes**	◼ **Mortar**
◼ **Wheelbarrows**	
◼ **Trowel**	
◼ **Screed**	
◼ **Stakes**	
◼ **Line level**	
◼ **Jointing tool**	
◼ **Whisk broom**	

3 *Embed the stones* in the mortar; then use a pointed trowel to fill the gaps with mortar.

courses. This is called "building the leads," and it ensures that the ends and corners will be plumb, square, and level.

To build a lead, trowel out a patch of mortar at the end or corner of the base course. Make sure that you use the best stones for the leads. Set the stones one course at a time. Allow the mortar to set up slightly; then tool the joints. **5**

This helps ensure that the mortar in the lower courses will be strong enough to hold the weight of the stones above. Check frequently with a mason's level to make sure that the lead faces are plumb and the courses are level.

smart tip

USING A GROUT BAG
A grout bag looks much the same as the pastry bags chefs use, but this heavy-duty version speeds up grout application and reduces clean up time as well. To use one, fill it with a slightly soupy grout mix; close the end; and squeeze to apply. The bag helps you get into tight spots with a minimum of mess.

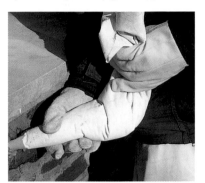

the Wall

1 *Do a dry run* before applying mortar. Use stones with flat faces for the first course.

2 *Spread a 2-in.-thick* layer of mortar about 3 ft. down the length of the wall.

4 *Set up stakes and string* to judge the evenness of the course. Use a line level on the string.

5 *Build up the leads* after laying the first course. Settle each stone in the mortar until level.

(Continued on page 162)

Fill in the Remaining Courses. After building up the leads, move the string lines up for the second course, again placing them about 3 inches higher than the desired top edge of the stones. As with the first course, test-fit the stones before applying mortar. Lay a 2-inch-thick bed of mortar, about 3 to 5 feet long, over the first course. Keep the mortar to within about 2 inches from the outside edges of the wall so that the mortar won't squeeze out when you set the stones. If it squeezes out, scrape it away with the trowel. Place bond stones every 4 to 6 feet, and use a level to check the wall frequently for plumb. **6**

Tool the Joints. After finishing each section, recess, or rake the outside joints to a depth of ½ to 1 inch. **7** Deep joints emphasize shadows and have a natural appearance. Shallow joints are better for walls made of semidressed and fully dressed cut stones.

Timing is critical when you tool the joints. The mortar should be set up enough so that pushing your thumb into it will barely leave a print (usually about 30 minutes after the stone was set).

Clean the Stone. After striking the joints for each section, use a whisk broom to remove

Constructing the Wall (Continued from page 161)

6 *Fill in the area* between the leads. Install bond stones every 4 to 6 ft.

7 *Tool the joints* as you complete each section of wall. Joints should be ½ to 1 in. deep.

9 *To cap a wall,* spread a thick layer of mortar over the top course of stone.

10 *Install the cap stones.* You can also top the wall with a mortar cap that crowns slightly.

smart tip

WEDGING UP IRREGULAR STONES

Some stones have surfaces that are too irregular to seat properly on the course below. Temporarily prop them into a level position with one or two small wooden wedges. Wet the wedges (so they will be easier to remove later), insert them, and mortar the joint. When the mortar is firm, pull out the wedges and fill the holes.

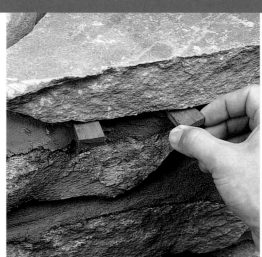

8 *Clean off loose mortar* with a stiff-bristle whisk broom as you work.

11 *Clean the finished wall* using water. For stubborn stains, clean with TSP.

loose mortar particles and smooth out the scraped joints. **8** Use a stiff-bristle brush to remove any mortar that has adhered to the face of the stone. A steel brush may work on some stones but may mar others; test in an inconspicuous area before using. If you've worked carefully while setting the stones, there shouldn't be much mortar to clean off.

Cap the Wall. Use the flattest, broadest, and best-looking stones for the top course, or cap. Or you can purchase quarried slabs to serve as a cap as shown here. Although this takes planning to find slabs that equal the width of your wall, this method provides a neat finished appearance that goes well with the rustic look of the stone wall.

Spread a 2-inch-thick layer of mortar over the top course. **9** Embed the cap stones in the mortar. **10** An alternative to cap stones is to finish off the top with a layer of solid mortar. The mortar cap should be 2 to 4 inches thick and crowned slightly to facilitate water runoff.

Clean the Wall. Once the mortar is hard, wash down the wall with clear water to remove any mortar stains. **11** If a mortar film still adheres to the stones, scrub the wall with a stiff brush and a mild detergent or a light solution of trisodium phosphate (TSP) and water. Wear rubber gloves when working with TSP.

1 Columns and pilasters built within a wall add design interest. They look best when spaced evenly down the length of the wall, a difficult task when using stones of different sizes.

2 Plan the placement of lighting fixtures, such as those shown here, carefully. Metal conduit holds the lighting cable inside the stone pillar. Install conduit higher than the wall, and then cut it when the wall is completed.

3 Here are two walls designed for different purposes. The tall wall in the background provides privacy for those using the pool. The short stone wall gradually gives way to a natural view.

4 Although difficult to build, a brick wall with spacings such as these seems to blend with the plantings more readily than a solid structure.

5 Rounded found stones, especially when the stones come from the local area, provide the materials for a rustic, naturalistic wall.

Gallery of
Wall Designs

Gallery of
Wall Designs

4

1 Even though it is only about waist-high to the average adult, the craftsmanship that went into building this wall makes it appear as an imposing barrier.

2 Stucco-covered block walls can resemble adobe walls. They are popular in the Southwest.

3 A tall brick wall serves as the backdrop for brick planters and brick stairs. The step-down design of the planter adds visual interest to the scheme.

4 Bond stones not only strengthen this wall, they extend beyond the wall to create an interesting design element.

5 A retaining wall made of fully-dressed stone lends a neat, crisp touch to this landscape.

6 Block and stucco does not need to be boring. If you're adding color to the stucco, choose a pigment that works with the surrounding foliage.

5

6

Concrete Block Walls

Types of Block

Basic Requirements

Building a Block Wall

Stucco Finishes

Concrete blocks provide a relatively fast, inexpensive means of building a sturdy masonry wall. It doesn't take many tools or skills to build a concrete-block wall. The large, uniform size of the blocks makes the work go quickly. Granted, you won't be able to build the wall as quickly as an experienced mason. However, you don't have to build the wall all at once. Because you're working with individual units, you can build the wall in stages.

Building concrete-block walls requires a lot of heavy lifting and hard work, so it's best to pace yourself according to your physical ability. Spend a few hours each evening after work, or spread the job out over several weekends.

Unlike stone walls, which are usually built with two stacks of stones, or wythes, a freestanding concrete-block wall can be built with a single stack of blocks. Walls up to 3 feet tall usually require no steel reinforcement, unless they serve as a retaining wall. (Higher walls require special techniques and are best left to professionals.)

Types of Blocks

Conventional concrete blocks are composed of portland cement, graded aggregate (crushed stone), and water. They weigh about 40 to 45 pounds each. The blocks are usually gray, although you can find them in several pastel or earth colors. Lighter-weight blocks, called cinder blocks, contain lightweight aggregate, such as expanded shale, clay, slate, or even pumice stone. Cinder blocks may be as light as 25 pounds. They are usually less expensive and easier to work with, but they don't have the structural strength and impact resistance of heavier blocks. Cinder blocks aren't recommended for building retaining walls or any wall that could be hit accidentally by a car or snow thrower. For building 3-foot garden walls, however, cinder blocks will usually suffice. Local building codes may limit their use.

Most blocks for walls have two or three hollow cores—called cells—to reduce their weight and to provide a place for rebar. The solid sections between the cores are called webs. On some blocks, the faces and webs are tapered to provide additional surface on the top of the block for mortar.

SHAPES AND SIZES

Standard concrete blocks have a nominal measurement of 8 x 8 x 16 inches long. The actual size is $7\frac{5}{8}$ x $7\frac{5}{8}$ x $15\frac{5}{8}$ inches to allow for a $\frac{3}{8}$-inch mortar joint. You use the (larger) nominal dimensions when estimating the number of blocks required for the job. Blocks also come in nominal widths of 4, 6, 8, 10, and 12 inches. Narrower sizes often are common in very low walls, planters, and garden borders.

Most wall construction involves two types of blocks—stretcher blocks and corner blocks. Stretcher blocks have two flanges at each end. Corner blocks have one flat end to provide a finished appearance at the ends or corners of a wall. Half blocks are half the length of a standard block and are also for building wall ends. Special solid-top blocks and cap blocks have smooth tops for finishing the top of the wall.

Specialty Blocks. Other specialty blocks are used for structural purposes in long or tall walls. Among these blocks are bond-beam blocks, pilaster (pier) blocks, and control-joint blocks. Bond-beam blocks have a U-shaped channel that you fill with mortar to strengthen the wall. Pilaster blocks are flat on both ends. Control-joint blocks have interlocking ends that are joined without mortar to allow for movement in the wall.

Decorative Blocks. You can also buy various types of decorative blocks, which have sculptured or patterned surfaces to add visual interest to the wall.

Screen blocks are narrow, lightweight blocks with patterned openings. The openings allow the passage of light and air through the wall while providing some privacy.

Because concrete blocks are manufactured locally, your choices will be limited to what's available at your local masonry supply or home center. Order decorative blocks or specialty blocks several weeks in advance.

TYPES OF BLOCK

Stretchers *have end flanges that butt in a mortar joint.*

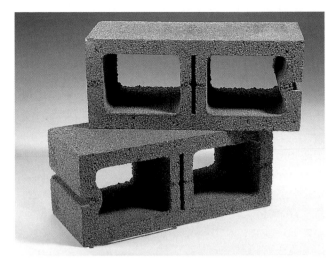

End blocks *have at least one finished end.*

Cap blocks *finish off the tops of block walls.*

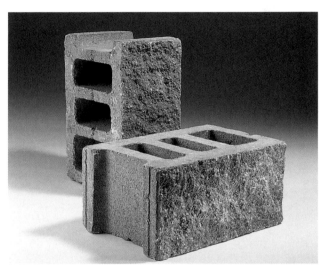

Rough-face blocks *offer a textured, stonelike surface.*

Interlocking blocks *are great for retaining walls.*

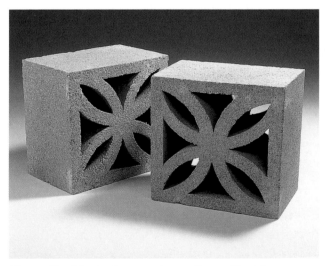

Decorative blocks *have webs on the vertical faces.*

11

Concrete Block Walls

ESTIMATING AMOUNTS

Base the number of blocks you'll need on the block's nominal dimensions, rather than on its actual dimensions. If possible, design the wall so that the height and length come out in multiples of the nominal dimensions of the blocks. For example, a standard block is nominally 8 x 8 x 16 inches, so a wall that's 8 inches wide, 32 inches high, and 8 feet long would require no cut blocks.

First, determine the length of the proposed wall in inches. Divide by the block length (typically 16 inches) to get the number of blocks needed for one course. Then divide the overall height of the wall by one block height (typically 8 inches) to determine the number of courses needed. To find out the total you'll need, multiply the blocks required along the length by the number of blocks required to create the height. Add 5 percent to allow for breakage. When figuring for walls with corners, measure the full length of each wall separately. A scale drawing of the wall will help you in your estimate. As a guide, plan on using about 113 standard-size blocks for every 100 square feet of wall.

Basic Requirements

Concrete-block walls need a poured-concrete footing for support. In some cases, reinforcement also may be needed. You can reinforce a wall by filling the cores with mortar and steel rods (called rebar) or by building a column (called a pilaster). Even low walls can fall apart if the cores aren't filled with concrete or if no rebar is used. Check local codes to see what's required in your area.

Footings and Foundations. Before you lay the first block, the footing must be poured, screeded, floated smooth, and allowed to cure fully. (See Chapter 9, "Wall Footings," beginning on page 146.) Pour the footing to the thickness required by local codes—typically 6 inches for 3-foot garden walls. To determine the required length of the footing, measure the

length of the proposed wall, and add 4 to 6 inches at each end. Typically, a footing is twice as wide as the block you'll be using.

If the top of the footing will be below the frost line, you can build a foundation up to ground level with stretchers and corner blocks. In some cases, the blocks below grade may need to be reinforced, usually by filling the block cavities with concrete or grout and inserting reinforcing rods. Check local codes for specific requirements in your area.

Mortar. Mortar for outdoor use is generally what is called Type N—1 part portland cement, 1 part hydrated lime, and 6 parts sand. For most residential wall projects, you're better off buying premixed mortar in sacks rather than mixing mortar from separate ingredients. Mortar mix should be somewhat drier than concrete. Test for proper amount by creating a series of ridges in the mixture with a hoe or shovel. If the ridges remain sharp and distinct, you have added the right amount of water.

If you're constructing a below-grade concrete-block foundation, Type M mortar may be required. (Type N weathers better; Type M produces a stronger bond.) Type M consists of 1 part portland cement, ¼ part hydrated lime, and 3 parts sand. Check local codes to see which mortar you should be using.

Control Joints. Control joints allow cracks to occur only at specific joints in the wall. On a small project, such as a short, low garden wall, you probably won't need control joints. However, long walls and those subject to unusual stresses will probably need control joints of some sort.

Because many variables determine how or where cracks may appear in a wall, there are no specific rules or guidelines on where control joints will be needed. Generally, cracks often occur at changes in wall height or at changes in footing level (such as above a stepped footing on hillside walls). Cracks may also occur at changes in wall thickness, such as at a pilaster. Long lengths of wall usually develop cracks due to uneven settling or movement of earth beneath the footing. As a rule of thumb, long walls should have control joints placed every 20 feet.

There are several ways you can incorporate control joints into a wall, but the easiest is to use special control-joint blocks. These are cast to form an interlocking tongue-and-groove joint. (The end of one block has a tongue, the other has a groove.) Lay half-size control-joint blocks every second course to create a straight control joint that runs from top to bottom of the wall. To allow for movement between the blocks, the joint is not mortared. Run a bead of flexible caulk into the control joint to hide the crack.

Tools. You need very few tools to lay a concrete-block wall. Tools and equipment used to mix and apply mortar include a mixer or mortar box, and a mortar board or hawk for carrying the mortar to the site. Use a medium pointing trowel for applying the mortar. Tap the blocks with the trowel's wooden handle to seat the blocks in the mortar bed. To aid in aligning blocks, you'll need a mason's line and wooden or plastic line blocks. You'll also need a level (at least 3 feet long) to level and plumb the blocks as you lay them. To finish the mortar joints, the most popular tool is a convex jointer,

Reinforcing Block Walls

VERTICAL Voids will align from top to bottom. Fill void every 4 ft. with concrete.

VERTICAL Drive rebar into the still-wet concrete. This provides top-to-bottom support.

HORIZONTAL On every other course, spread a layer of mortar.

HORIZONTAL Set block reinforcement wire into the mortar.

which makes an indented joint that sheds water.

Cutting Concrete Blocks. If the length of the wall isn't an exact multiple of the block length plus mortar joints, you will have to cut the blocks. The most accurate way to cut concrete blocks is with a masonry saw (available at tool rentals) or a portable circular saw fitted with a masonry blade or abrasive disc. If you have only a few blocks to cut, use a brick hammer and mason's chisel or brick set. Mark both sides of the block; then tap the chisel along the line.

Bond Patterns. Most standard blocks are laid in a simple running-bond pattern, in which the joints of each successive course are staggered by exactly half a block. This pattern provides the greatest strength, and it makes the best use of standard block sizes with a minimum amount of cut blocks. You can add interest to a bond pattern by combining blocks of varying sizes. Other patterns include an offset bond and a stacked bond. A stacked bond, with one joint directly above the next, is common on screen-block walls. It isn't as structurally sound as the others, so it usually requires vertical reinforcement.

Building a Block Wall

The following steps show how to lay the first course of a concrete-block wall. The instructions assume that you have already placed a suitable poured-concrete footing. You also should have the ingredients and tools for mixing mortar. As mentioned, concrete blocks do not need to be wet down before being laid.

Mark the Wall Ends or Corners. First, locate the outside corners or ends of the wall by stretching lines between the batter boards that you set up for the footing. On straight walls, hang a plumb bob at the wall's ends. If your wall has corners, hang it from the intersecting lines as well. Mark these spots on the footing with a pencil.

With a helper, snap chalk lines on the footing to represent the outside edges of each wall. Starting at one end or corner, make a trial run, laying the entire first course along the chalk lines. **1** Place ⅜-inch wood spacers between the blocks to represent mortar joints. If possible, adjust the mortar joint spacing slightly so that you don't have to cut blocks. If you have to cut

blocks, they must be at least one-half block long. Fill smaller spaces by cutting two blocks: for a space that is a one-quarter-block long, for example, cut two blocks to five-eighths their full length. Remove a block next to the gap. Fill the resulting gap with the cut blocks. Once all the blocks are laid out, check the corners to make sure that they meet at 90 degrees.

Spread the Mortar. Remove the blocks, and stand them on end as close as possible to where they will be laid. Mix a stiff batch of mortar; then starting at one corner, lay a continuous mortar bed about 1-inch thick along one of the chalk lines. Keep the edge of the mortar bed about ½ inch inside the chalk lines so that you don't cover them. Put down enough mortar to set three or four blocks. Hold the trowel at an angle so that the edge smoothes and flattens the mortar. Then use the point of the tool to create a series of shallow ridges or furrows in the mortar. The weight of the block will squeeze out the furrows and spread the mortar thoroughly over the blocks.

SET THE FIRST BLOCK

Set the end or corner block on the mortar bed, aligned with the chalk lines on the footing. Embed the block in the mortar by tapping on the top lightly with the trowel handle. Place a level, both crosswise and lengthwise, on top of the block to make sure it is level in all directions. **2** Make adjustments by tapping on the block with the trowel handle. Then use a measuring tape, folding rule, or a story pole to check the block height. The top of a standard block should be exactly 8 inches above the footing. If the block is too high, tap it down with the trowel handle; if the block is too low, remove it and add more mortar.

Add Stretcher Blocks. With your trowel, swipe a ¾-inch-thick layer of mortar on the two flanges, or ears, at one end of a stretcher block. **3** Grasp the top web opening, and lift the block just over its location on the mortar bed. Gently but quickly set the block in the mortar bed; nudge it against the corner block; and seat

CUTTING CONCRETE BLOCK
You can purchase half blocks to create staggered joints in the courses, but sometimes you will need to trim a block. The easiest way is to use a circular saw with a masonry cutting blade. Be sure to wear eye protection when cutting any type of masonry.

it by tapping it with the trowel handle. If the mortar falls off, remove the block and try again. Measure the mortar joint, and tap the block closer to its neighbor if necessary. Use a level to make sure the block is level in both directions and that the tops and faces of the blocks are in alignment. Repeat this procedure with the third block. If you're building a corner, lay blocks at right angles to the corner block and check for square. After laying each block, clean excess mortar off the footing with a trowel. After you set three blocks, go to the opposite end of the wall and set three blocks there.

Fill in the Remaining Blocks. Attach line blocks—often given away when you buy block—to the two end blocks. Stretch string between them, and tighten it to hold the blocks in place. Position the string even with the top of the concrete blocks and level the string with a line level. The blocks should be level with each other. If there is only a slight difference, make succeeding mortar joints thicker or thinner on one end of the wall until both sides are level. If they aren't level, use mortar to make them level.

Once these blocks are level, use the string as a guide to fill in the remaining blocks in the first course.

Building a Block Wall

TOOLS

- Work gloves
- Safety glasses
- Pencil
- Shovels and tamper
- Level
- Mason's block and string
- Hammer and brick set
- Trowels and striking tool
- Wheelbarrow or mixer
- Bucket

MATERIALS

- Concrete blocks
- Mortar
- Wire lath
- Rebar (optional)
- Concrete and gravel (for footing)

1 *Place the first course* as a trial run. You may need to adjust the blocks to avoid awkward cuts.

2 *Spread a 1-in.-thick* bed of mortar, and place the first block. Check for level.

3 *Butter the blocks* as you install them by placing mortar on the end of each flange.

(Continued on page 176)

Set the Closure Block. This is the last block to be set in the course and is often the most difficult to lay because it must fit neatly between two blocks. First, measure the opening to determine whether a full-size block will fit. If not, you'll need to cut the block. Swipe mortar onto the ends of the last block and onto the blocks on either side of the opening in the wall. Slowly slide the block into place. **4** Make sure enough mortar remains in the joints to make a tight seal. If a small amount of mortar falls out, leave the block in place and tuck more mortar into the joint with your trowel. With the first course finished, check for level.

Build Corner Leads. Once they've laid the first course, most masons build the leads—the corners or ends—before laying the next course. They set as many blocks as it takes to end up with a single block at the top course.

Start by applying a 1-inch-thick layer of mortar on the top edges of the first few blocks of the first course. For most low garden walls, you need only mortar the outer edges of the block (called face-shell mortaring). For a stronger installation, you can mortar the webbing between the cores (called full mortaring). If you're building a wall that stops instead of turning a corner, start the second course with a half block.

Building a Block Wall (Continued from page 175)

4 *After buttering edges,* slowly slide the closure block in place to complete the first course.

5 *After installing the first course,* build up the leads or corners of the wall.

8 *To guide installation* of the stretcher blocks, align each course to a level string.

9 *Control joints* keep adjoining blocks from being mortared together. Fill spaces with flexible caulk.

Press the block for the second course into the mortar bed, aligned with the blocks beneath it. **5** Tap the block level with your trowel handle, and check the height. Continue laying up blocks to build a lead with a single block at the top. Check frequently to see that the blocks are level, plumb, and aligned. **6** As you build up the lead, check the alignment of the bond pattern by holding a straightedge diagonally across the top corners of the blocks. **7**

Fill in Stretcher Courses. After building each end or corner lead, fill in the stretcher courses between them. For each course, attach the line block to the corner blocks. Align the string with the top edge of the blocks. **8**

Long walls will require control joints. The joint relieves the stresses that build up in the wall. You can buy control-joint blocks or install felt paper between blocks. **9** The paper prevents the joint from being mortared. When the wall is finished, fill the joint with caulk.

Tooling the Joints. As you work, remove excess mortar with a trowel. **10** After about 20 or 30 minutes, press a mortar joint with your thumb. If a print remains but the mortar does not stick to your thumb, shape the joint. **11**

6 **As you construct the lead,** check frequently to make sure the blocks are plumb.

7 **Check the alignment** of the lead by holding a straightedge on the corners of the blocks.

10 **As you work,** remove excess mortar with a trowel. Keep blocks as clean as possible.

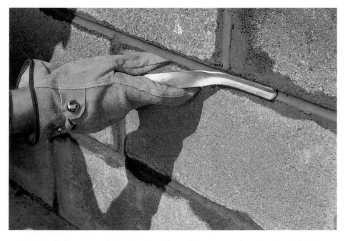

11 **Concave joints** shed water; create flush joints for walls that will be covered with stucco.

Concrete Block Walls

11

(Continued on page 178)

Cap the Wall. You can cap the wall in one of several ways. The simplest method involves mortaring solid cap blocks on top of the wall. Another option is to fill the top block cores with mortar and create a mortared top. If you do this, cover the cores in the next-to-last course with metal screen. **12** The screen, available from masonry suppliers, keeps the mortar from falling down into the blocks below. Fill the cores in the top course with concrete or mortar, and strike it flush. **13** For a cap, trowel out a few feet of mortar and set the cap. **14** An alternative is to set stones in mortar. **15**

smart tip

PAINTING BLOCK WALLS
If you want to paint a block wall, be sure to wait until the mortar has cured completely—about five to seven days. Scrub all surfaces with a solution of 1 cup trisodium phosphate (TSP) to 1 gallon of water to remove grease, oil, mortar smears, and minor efflorescence. Rinse thoroughly and allow to dry. Choose paint recommended for exterior masonry surfaces. Because masonry walls are relatively rough, use a long-nap roller and apply at least two coats of paint.

Building a Block Wall (Continued from page 177)

12 **Cover the tops,** of the last-to-next course with wire mesh to hold the mortar.

13 **Lay the top course,** and fill all of the voids with mortar.

14 **For a finished appearance,** install cap blocks set in mortar along the top of the wall.

15 **An alternative treatment** is to set small cut stones in a bed of mortar.

Stucco Finishes

Bare concrete-block walls aren't very attractive, no matter how you've designed and built them. At the very least, you'll probably want to give them a coat of paint. Other treatments for masonry walls include stucco and brick or stone veneers.

Stucco is a popular and attractive surfacing material. Many different textures and effects are possible: rough textures tend to hide minor imperfections on wall surfaces. (See "Fancy Finishes," page 181.) Usually, stucco is applied in its natural gray color and painted later, but color powder may be mixed into the stucco before application. If applied properly, stucco makes a durable surface coating that can be used in many climates. However, stucco work takes considerable skill, and once you start applying a coat of stucco, you must finish the entire surface. If you wish to tackle the job, here are a few guidelines for applying stucco to a new concrete-block wall.

APPLYING STUCCO

If you are planning to stucco a concrete-block wall, strike the mortar joints flush as you build. Then you can apply stucco directly to the wall in either two or three coats. Either way, the first coat is the scratch coat; it literally gets scratched to receive the second coat. The second coat is called the brown coat. It is mixed and applied the same way as the scratch coat. The optional third coat is the finish coat. It's a thinner coat made of white cement and white stucco sand for a white appearance. Or, you can add color pigment to the mix. The pigment is available in a variety of earth tones. The wall should be clean and damp (but not wet) before applying stucco. The project shown is a two-coat stucco wall.

Prepare the Wall. Clean the wall. Install base strip bead to keep the stucco off of the ground. Attach a corner bead if your wall turns the corner. Make up a mix of 1 part mortar cement and 4 parts sand, and add just enough water to make the mix workable.

Prepare the Scratch Coat. Start at the bottom of the wall, and using a flat, square trowel, apply a ¼-inch-thick coat of stucco over the surface. **1**

Stucco Walls

TOOLS	MATERIALS
■ Work gloves	■ Masonry bonding agent
■ Cold chisel and hammer	■ Base and corner bead
■ Wire brush	■ Masonry nails
■ Mixing tray	■ Stucco mix
■ Spray bottle	■ Plastic sheeting
■ Level	
■ Trowels	
■ Raking tool	
■ Finishing float	

1 *Attach metal base* strip and corner bead to the wall. Apply a ¼-in. coat of stucco.

smart tip

MAKE A RAKING TOOL
Cut a length of 1x2 and hammer in galvanized roofing nails every ¾ in.

(Continued on page 180)

11
concrete Block walls

This coat is scratched to provide a good bond for the next coat. As soon as you have finished an area, roughen it with a plasterer's rake, or make your own scratching tool. The scratches should run horizontally about ½ to ¾ inches apart, and should be about ⅛ inch deep. **2**

Second Coat. If you are applying three coats, the second coat is called the brown coat. The brown coat is made of the same mixture of sand and mortar as the scratch coat, unless you're using it as the top coat. Keeping the delay between the two coats to a minimum makes for the strongest bond: apply the brown coat as soon as the scratch coat will accept it without cracking. If you must wait longer, spray the scratch coat with a fine mist of water. Once you've applied the brown coat, allow the wall to cure for a few days, keeping it moist.

Apply the Finish Coat. Make the white coat from 1 part white cement and 3 parts white stucco sand. You can add a powder color agent to the mix if you wish to create a unique design. It's best to test your colors on a small section. Moisten the wall. **3** Using a flat steel trowel, apply a ⅛- to ¼-inch coat. **4** Cover the wall with plastic sheeting to allow the stucco to cure. **5**

Stucco Over a Block Wall *(Continued from page 179)*

2 *Scratch the first coat* to provide tooth for the next coat you apply.

3 *After the scratch coat* has set up, spray it down with water to help the final coat adhere.

4 *Apply the finish coat* with a trowel, smoothing it to a ¼-in.-thick coat.

5 *Clean excess mortar,* and cover the wall with plastic for 48 hours to allow the stucco cure.

FANCY FINISHES

FLOATED SMOOTH

SPONGE SWIRLED

BRUSH LINED

BRUSH SPLATTERED

FLATTENED SPLATTER

BOARD DRAGGED

TROWEL SWIRLED

TROWEL RIDGED

11

Concrete Block Walls

Brick Walls

rick is one of the most attractive materials you can use to build a wall, and it comes in a variety of sizes, colors, and surface textures. You can set it in many different bond patterns and finish the joints in a number of different profiles.

A typical wall is either one brick thick, known as single wythe, or two bricks thick, known as double wythe. Usually, brick walls under 2 feet high require no steel reinforcement. Taller walls may incorporate steel ties or even metal reinforcement into the design to withstand stresses and loads placed on the wall. Consult your local building department for structural requirements.

Types of Bricks

Many different types of bricks are available, but those used for walls fall into three broad cate-gories: building brick, face brick, and concrete brick. Within each of these categories, you'll find a wide variety of sizes, shapes, colors, and surface textures.

Building Brick. Also called common brick, building bricks are economical and are suitable for building low, informal garden walls. They may be a bit too rustic where a neat, formal look is desired. Building bricks are usually the "seconds" or "rejects" from the brickyard. Some bricks may be chipped, warped, or broken. Color, dimensions, and density may vary from brick to brick.

Face Brick. If a neat appearance is important, use face bricks. Compared with building brick, face brick is uniform in size, color, and surface texture. Face bricks come in a great variety of colors and textures and are the standard brick used in most outdoor construction. They're more expensive than building bricks, but because they're more uniform in size and shape, they're easier to work with than building brick. They also have a better finished appearance and are suitable for formal projects.

Concrete Brick. As the name implies, these bricks are formed from concrete. They cost considerably less than either type of clay brick. Concrete bricks are similar in appearance to concrete blocks, with a slightly rougher, more porous surface than clay bricks. Colors usually are limited to light or medium brick red or adobe beige. Concrete bricks don't have the strength of clay bricks, so they are prone to cracking, especially under severe freeze-thaw conditions. Check with your local

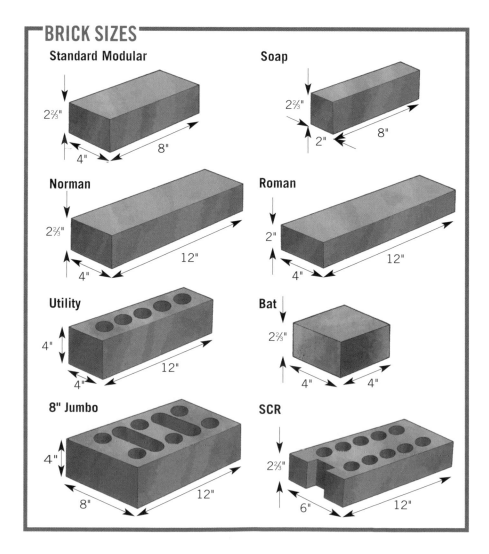

BRICK SIZES

Standard Modular
$2\frac{2}{3}$" 4" 8"

Soap
$2\frac{2}{3}$" 2" 8"

Norman
$2\frac{2}{3}$" 4" 12"

Roman
2" 4" 12"

Utility
4" 4" 12"

Bat
$2\frac{2}{3}$" 4" 4"

8" Jumbo
4" 8" 12"

SCR
$2\frac{2}{3}$" 6" 12"

Right Although brick is a rigid material, it is possible to create sweeping curves. Consider tall walls as a backdrop for plantings as well as privacy.

building department to see whether these bricks are recommended for your particular project. If you use concrete bricks, plan to seal them with a waterproof masonry sealer. Ask the dealer for the appropriate product.

BRICK SIZES

Most bricks come in modular sizes. The length of the most common modular unit, a standard brick, is roughly twice its width and three times its thickness. The nominal dimensions are 2⅔x4x8 inches. The actual brick is smaller than this by the thickness of a mortar joint—either ⅜ inch or ½ inch. Size varies for another reason, too: manufacturing tolerances. In any given production run, brick sizes can vary as much as ½ inch. If you're concerned about size, ask the dealer for the dimensions of the brick you intend to use. Other types of bricks used in wall construction include jumbo, Roman, Norman, SCR, and utility.

Some bricks used for walls have hollow cores to reduce their weight, provide a better mortar bond, and allow space to insert vertical reinforcing rods when constructing a tall wall, when required. While hollow-core bricks are sometimes less expensive than solid ones, you generally have fewer choices in size, color, and surface texture.

Types of Walls

Besides the look of the bricks themselves, two factors determine a brick wall's appearance. One is the number of wythes used to build up the wall thickness; the other is the bond pattern in which you lay the bricks.

Wythes. A wall that is only one brick wide (4 inches wide if using standard bricks) is called a single-wythe wall. When a second, parallel course of bricks is added next to the first, you have a double-wythe wall. A double-wythe wall is stronger than a single wythe, and the thicker wall may look more appropriate with other landscape features. Depending on the desired overall width of the wall, the wythes may be butted together (with a mortar joint between wythes) to produce a wall 8 inches wide or spaced apart to provide additional width. In the latter case, the cavity between the two wythes may be filled with grout (thinned mortar) or concrete (and sometimes reinforcing rods) to provide additional strength for tall walls. In all cases, the two wythes are tied together, either by bricks (called headers), metal masonry ties, or a combination of these, depending on the bond pattern. (For more on tying wythes together, see "Reinforcement," page 188.)

Bond Patterns. The drawing opposite shows the popular running-bond pattern for brick walls. Some patterns—such as the common bond, Flemish bond, and English bond—are structural bonds. They incorporate header bricks to tie the wythes together. Running-bond and stack-bond usually require metal masonry ties to reinforce the wall. Single-wythe walls typically use a running-bond, offset running-bond, or stack-bond pattern. In the first two, the vertical joints are offset to provide additional strength. In a stack bond (also called Jack-on-Jack), the bricks are simply stacked one atop the other so that all vertical joints are aligned. A stack bond has virtually no lateral strength, depending almost entirely on the strength of the mortar joints to hold it together. Such walls are typically reinforced with masonry ties in horizontal joints. If vertical reinforcement is needed, use hollow-core bricks and insert rebar into the cores, as required by code. Check with your local building department for specific requirements.

ANATOMY OF A BRICK WALL

As in other trades, brick masons have terms to describe the components of their handiwork, in this case a brick wall. Learning these terms will help you understand the instructions in this chapter. One horizontal row of bricks is called a course. The courses are identified as odd courses (first, third, fifth course, etc.) and even courses (second, fourth, sixth course, etc.), starting from the base of the wall up. When building the wall, you'll get the best results by building the ends of the wall (the leads) first, rather than laying complete courses from one end of the wall to the other. Leads help establish proper alignment of vertical mortar joints and let you attach a mason's line at each end to keep the wall straight and level. The last brick you lay in each course is called the closure brick. Even if you take considerable care in laying out the wall, the closure bricks often must be cut to fit.

Stretchers and Headers. Stretchers are bricks laid flat with the long dimension parallel with the length of the wall. If the brick is laid on edge, it's called a rowlock stretcher. Headers are bricks laid flat at right angles to the stretchers, tying the two wythes together. A header laid on edge becomes a rowlock header. Header courses are often used to cap the wall as well.

Bats and Soaps. Bats are bricks cut in half across their width. Bricks cut along their length are called soaps. Both are sometimes available precut, but more likely, you'll need to cut them yourself. Commonly, bats are used in single-wythe walls to finish the ends and to produce various patterns.

Head Joints and Bed Joints. Vertical mortar joints between bricks are called head joints; horizontal joints between courses are called bed joints.

ESTIMATING AMOUNTS

Bricks are more expensive than most other masonry products. You buy bricks by the piece. You may get a discount if you buy a whole pallet. As with lumber, you can sometimes go into the yard and hand-pick bricks out of the pile, if you want. Generally, if you're building a wall that requires hundreds or thousands of bricks, you order more than you need (to compensate for breakage and other waste) and have the bricks delivered.

The number of bricks you'll need to build a wall depends on the size of the wall, the number of wythes, the size of individual bricks, mortar-joint spacing, and the bond pattern. Bond patterns that include header bricks will require more bricks than those that use only stretchers.

A simple way to calculate the number of bricks you'll need is to make a scale elevation drawing for a 2- to 4-foot section of the wall you're building. In your drawing, include the bond pattern and the overall height of the wall. Draw in the bricks at their nominal, rather than actual size, and you'll be able to leave the mortar joints out of your drawing. Count the bricks in the section, and multiply the number of bricks required for each section by the number of sections required to complete the wall. Add 5 to 10 percent extra to allow for miscuts, breakage, and future repairs.

ANATOMY OF A BRICK WALL

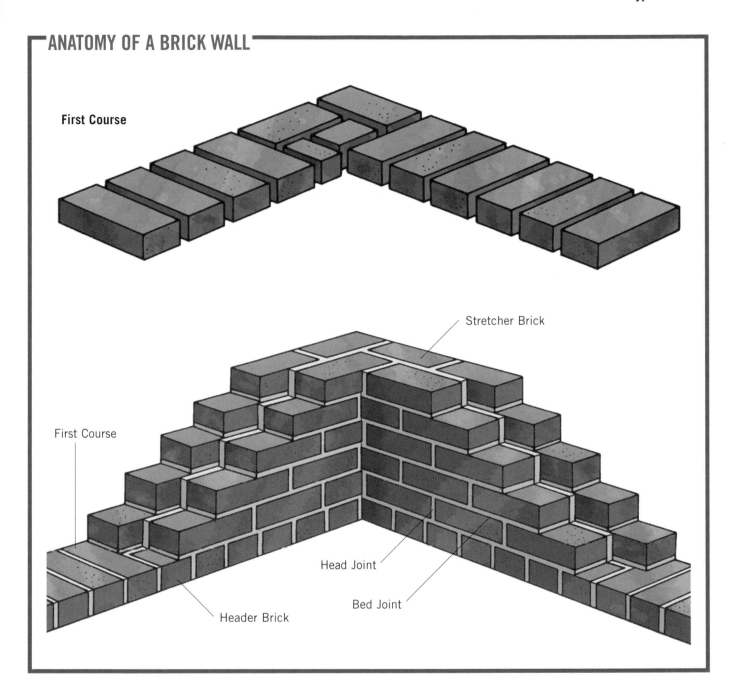

First Course

Stretcher Brick

First Course

Head Joint

Bed Joint

Header Brick

Basic Requirements

Building a sturdy brick wall depends on three factors: a strong footing, adequate reinforcement, and proper mortar mix to bond the bricks together. Lacking any one of these elements, the wall will soon crack and eventually fall apart.

FOOTINGS

As a rule, a poured-concrete footing should be two times wider than the wall it supports and as thick as the wall is wide. The footing should also extend 4 to 6 inches beyond the ends of the wall. In severe winter climates, the footing must be below the frost line which may be 36 inches or more. You can build the foundation up to ground level with concrete blocks. Usually, the top of the footing or foundation will be a few inches below grade, where it won't be seen. Fill the foundation-block cavities with mortar, and insert reinforcing rods.

Be sure to check local codes for specific footing and foundation requirements. (Complete instructions for constructing footings appear in Chapter 9, beginning on page 146.)

REINFORCEMENT

Requirements for wall reinforcement will vary depending on wall height, bond pattern, soil stability, wind load, and other factors. Check with your building department for accepted practices and code requirements for your particular project. For most walls up to 3 feet high, a structural bond pattern, such as common bond, provides sufficient strength, so no additional reinforcement will be needed. Walls set in a stacked-bond or running-bond pattern are usually tied together with metal Z-ties embedded in the mortar, as shown in the drawing below. Tall walls may also require reinforcement with metal rebar as shown opposite.

Z-Ties. Steel Z-ties are used to tie wythes together in a double-wythe wall. Typically, the ties are placed in a bed joint spaced 36 inches apart (or as required by code) along every third or fourth course. Stagger the ties so that they do not align vertically.

Reinforcement Bar. Steel bars, known as "rebar," come in many different diameters and are designated by a number, such as #3, #4, etc. These numbers correspond to $\frac{1}{8}$-inch increments: #3 rebar is $\frac{3}{8}$ inch in diameter, #4 is $\frac{1}{2}$ inch in diameter, and so on. Rebar is inserted

into the concrete footing; it extends up between wythes in a double-wythe wall or through brick cores in a single-wythe wall. You can cut rebar with a hacksaw.

Pilasters. Pilasters, or built-in columns, are sometimes incorporated into brick walls to provide additional strength. Typically, the pilasters are located at both ends or corners and at 10- to 12-foot intervals along the length of the wall. The use of pilasters is especially recommended for single-wythe walls.

Pilasters are tied into the wall with header bricks and Z-ties. In double-wythe walls, the cavity in the pilaster is filled with grout (mortar that has been thinned so it can be poured) or concrete and reinforced with rebar. In all cases, the poured concrete footing should follow the shape of the pilasters. Consult your building department to see whether pilasters are required for your wall design and which type is recommended. Even if they aren't required, pilasters can lend visual interest to a wall. Several basic designs are shown in the drawing.

MORTAR

Mortar is a mixture of cement, hydrated lime, sand, and water. Type N mortar is most often used for freestanding brick garden walls. How-

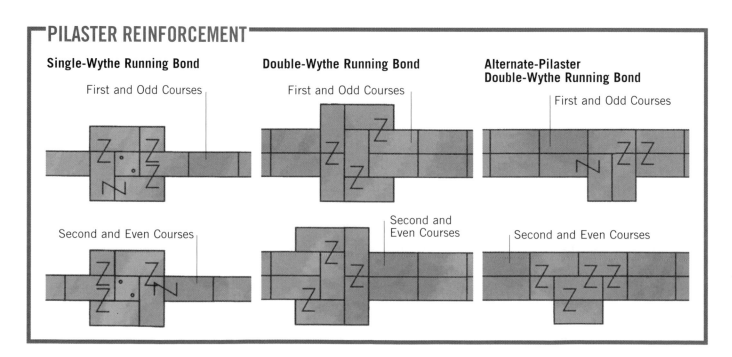

PILASTER REINFORCEMENT

Single-Wythe Running Bond
First and Odd Courses
Second and Even Courses

Double-Wythe Running Bond
First and Odd Courses
Second and Even Courses

Alternate-Pilaster
Double-Wythe Running Bond
First and Odd Courses
Second and Even Courses

MortarTypes

Type	Proportions of Ingredients	Recommended for:
M	1 Cement ¼ Hydrated lime 3 Sand	Foundations, walks, retaining walls, and wherever masonry will have a long-term contact with damp earth.
S	1 Cement ¼-½ Hydrated lime 4½ Sand	Reinforced masonry and wherever high-bond strength is needed, such as walls in windy areas.
N	1 Cement ¼-½ Hydrated lime 6 Sand	Weather-exposed structures, such as above-grade garden walls.

WALL REINFORCEMENT

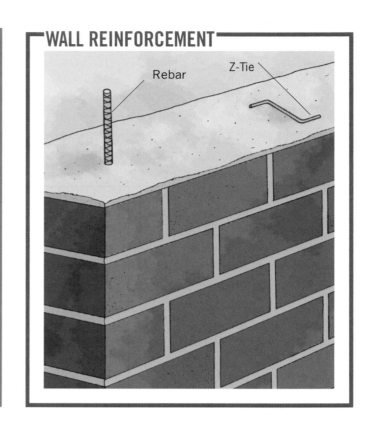

Rebar   Z-Tie

ever, you should consult a local masonry dealer for the best type to use. As a rule, increasing the proportions of lime and sand in relationship to cement makes mortar less expensive and more workable, but weaker. The table above shows mortar mixtures and their applications.

For most residential walls, it's more convenient to buy premixed mortar in bags than to mix the components yourself. A 70-pound bag of premixed mortar is enough to set about 40 standard bricks.

Mortar Consistency. As with bagged dry-mix concrete, you'll need to add the correct amount of water to achieve the desired consistency. This may take some experimentation. Generally, stiffer mixes are used for concrete block, while wetter mixes are used for bricks. You can mix mortar with a shovel or hoe in a wheelbarrow, in a concrete barge, or on a large sheet of plywood. A power mixer is recommended for large jobs to speed the mixing and to save your back. Work in small batches at first. If the mortar starts to dry out, you can add a bit more water to bring it back to the proper consistency. This process, called "retempering the mortar," can be done only one time for each batch. Additional retempering severely weakens the mix.

Grout. Grout is thin, pourable mortar. It's made by adding enough water to the mortar mix to make it soupy. You can use grout, and sometimes vertical rebar, to fill the cavity between a double-wythe wall. Pour the grout as you work: after laying several courses of a wall, pour grout into the cavity with a coffee can. Then lay a few more courses. Repeat the process to the full height of the wall. Whether or not you need to add grout or other reinforcement depends on soil conditions and the wall's function and design. Check with your building department.

smart tip

CARRYING TOOL
Brick tongs come in handy when you have to carry a number of bricks from one spot to another. They consist of a sliding clamp and a handle.

Building a Single-Wythe Wall

The following steps show how to lay a single-wythe brick wall in a running-bond pattern. The instructions assume that you have already poured a suitable footing and will be providing any reinforcement required by local building codes. Unlike concrete blocks, bricks need to be dampened before you lay them. Dry bricks absorb moisture from the mortar joint, resulting in a poor bond. Thoroughly spray all the bricks in the pile with a garden hose an hour or two before laying them. By the time you get the mortar mixed, the surface water should have evaporated from the bricks, leaving them slightly damp. Do not lay the bricks if they are dripping wet.

WALL LAYOUT

For straight walls with no corners, you can simply mark the center of the footing and center the wall on the mark. On walls that turn a corner, lay out the wall with the help of the batter boards you set up for the footing. Stretch string across the batter boards to mark the outside of the wall. Where strings intersect at corners, drop a plumb bob from the intersecting lines and mark this point on the footing. Snap chalk lines on the footing to represent the outside wall edges.

Do a Trial Run. Starting at one end or corner, dry lay the first course along the chalk line. Place ½-inch wood spacers between the bricks to represent mortar joints. You may want to adjust the joint widths slightly to avoid cutting a brick. Do not, however, make joints narrower than ⅜ inch or wider than ⅝ inch. If you must cut a brick, try to make it a bat (half brick), and place it at the end of the wall. After the course is laid, remove the wood spacers. Mark every joint with a pencil; then set the bricks aside where they'll be within easy reach as you lay up the wall. **1**

Spread the Mortar. Mix a batch of mortar; then starting at one corner, lay a 1-inch-thick mortar bed long enough to place four or five bricks, but slightly narrower than the width of a brick. **2** Be careful not to cover the chalk lines. On second and subsequent courses, use your trowel to make a furrow down the center of the mortar bed so that the edges are thicker than the center.

Set the First Bricks. Set the end or corner brick in the mortar even with the chalk lines. Embed

Building a Single-Wythe Wall

TOOLS

- ◼ Work gloves
- ◼ String and stakes
- ◼ Tools for mixing mortar
- ◼ Trowels
- ◼ Levels
- ◼ Hammer and cold chisel
- ◼ Striking tool

MATERIALS

- ◼ Concrete for footing
- ◼ Mortar
- ◼ Brick

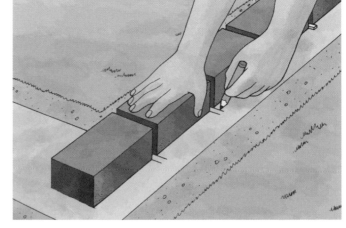

1 *Lay out a course without mortar,* using wood as spacers. Mark mortar joints with a pencil.

the brick by tapping on the top lightly with the trowel handle until the mortar joint compresses to ½ inch. Check to see that the brick is level. Swipe a ¾-inch layer of mortar on one end of the next brick; place it on the mortar bed about 1 to 2 inches away from the corner brick; and slide it in place with a slight downward motion.

A small amount of mortar should squeeze out of the joints. With the edge of the trowel, scrape off any squeezed-out mortar and reuse it. Set two or three more bricks in this fashion; then move to the opposite end of the wall, and repeat the process.

Check Your Work. Check with a level to make sure all the bricks are aligned. If a brick is too high, tap it down with the trowel handle. **3** If a brick is too low, remove it and add more mortar. Once you've trued up the two ends of the wall, attach a string to line blocks at the ends of the wall. Position the string even with the tops of the bricks, and check the string with a line level. It is important that the bricks at each end be level with each other. If they are slightly out of level (less than about ¾ inch), trowel mortar under the low end and reset the bricks. If the bricks are more than ¾ inch out of level, compensate by laying thicker bed joints at the low

end over several courses. Eventually the level should even out.

Build the End Leads. For a straight wall with no corners, build the leads. Working from the end, lay three bricks; lay two bricks on top of them; and then set a single brick at the very top. (When you've got the experience, you can build a lead as many as five courses high.) If Z-ties are required, insert these in the horizontal joints.

smart tip

MAKE A STORY POLE
Use a story pole to check your work as you build the wall. Make the pole from a straight 1x4, and use a brick as a guide for drawing the lines on the board. Don't forget to draw lines for the mortar joints as well.

12

Brick Walls

2 *Lay a 1-in.-thick* bed of mortar. Make the mortar edges thicker than the center for top courses.

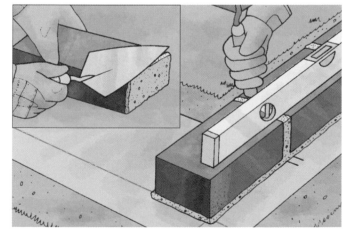

3 *Apply mortar* to the edges of the the bricks. Check your work with a level as you work.

(Continued on page 192)

Tooling Mortar Joints

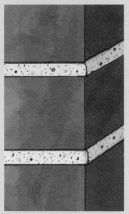

Extruded joint

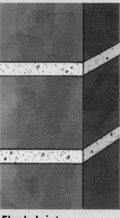

Flush Joint

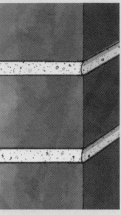

Concave Joint

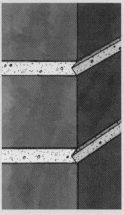

V-Joint

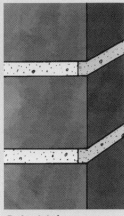

Raked Joint

EXTRUDED JOINTS. Extruded joints require no tooling; they are formed naturally as mortar squeezes out between the bricks when you tap them in place. Such joints are used where a rustic appearance or texture is desired, but they tend to trap water, making them relatively weak. Also, pieces of mortar tend to break away, leaving an unattractive finish. Using a masonry sealer will help extend the life of these joints. (Ask your masonry dealer for the appropriate product.)

FLUSH JOINTS. To create a flush joint, simply cut away the excess mortar with the edge of your trowel as you lay the bricks. Flush joints produce a smooth surface and are often used for brick walls that will be painted or stuccoed. Left

unpainted, the joints are not particularly watertight, and surface layers may eventually flake off or crack.

CONCAVE JOINTS. These joints are the most popular because they shed water well. To make these joints, press a convex jointer into the mortar and slide it along the joint. The tool compresses the mortar, making a strong, watertight joint. Walls with concave joints have a flat look, with little or no shadow.

V-JOINTS. These joints are made by removing mortar with a pointed tool called a V-jointer. V-joints emphasize shadows and allow good water runoff, making them relatively watertight joints.

Building a Single-Wythe Wall

4 *As you build out the leads,* check the wall height and bond alignment frequently.

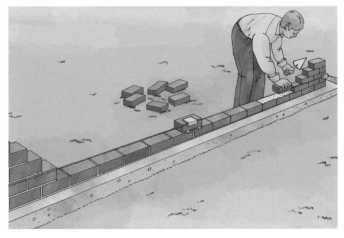

5 *After completing* a few courses of the leads, fill in the bricks between the leads.

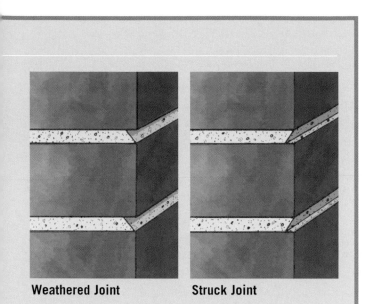

Weathered Joint   Struck Joint

RAKED JOINTS. These joints are recessed about ½ inch back from the face of the wall, using a tool called a rake-out jointer. Raked joints create dark shadows for a dramatic effect. However, they collect water and may encourage the growth of moss in the mortar joints, which will eventually crack or erode them. Avoid this joint in damp areas.

WEATHERED JOINTS AND STRUCK JOINTS. Make these by removing mortar with the point of a mason's trowel. Orient the trowel tip upward for weathered joints, downward for struck joints. Both joints produce attractive shadow line. For practical purposes, weathered joints shed water better than struck joints.

(Continued from page 190)

6 *Use mason's blocks* and string to keep the level of each course true.

Build up the leads three to five courses high before you fill in the center sections of the courses. **4** Check course heights with a tape measure or a story pole. (See "Make a Story Pole," page 191.) Check the leads for plumb and level frequently. Hold the level diagonally across the corners of the bricks as shown. The level should touch each brick to make sure the corners align. If it doesn't, adjust the width of your head joints.

Fill in Between Leads. Attach line blocks to the second course of bricks in each lead, aligning the string with the top edge of the bricks. If the line has to reach a long distance, it may sag, so temporarily support it in the middle with a brick. **5** Use wood spacers to raise the brick ½ inch to simulate a mortar bed, and if necessary, place a fold of flashing over the brick to hold the string in place.

The last brick in each course is called a closure brick and must fit neatly between the two bricks on either side, so careful planning and measuring is important. If possible, plan the job so that you can use a full-size brick for the closure brick.

Lay the Rest of the Bricks. Set the rest of the brick courses to fill in between the leads. **6** For the best appearance, stagger the closure bricks so that they do not align vertically. Build new leads once you've filled in between existing ones and repeat the process until the wall is complete.

Finish the Mortar Joints. As you work, use your trowel to smooth any squeezed-out mortar flush along the joints. Keep your eye on the joints as you work, and test them by pressing your thumb gently into the mortar. If your thumbprint remains and the mortar doesn't stick to your hand, then it's time to tool the mortar joints. Select the appropriate tool for the type of joint you want to make. (See "Tooling Mortar Joints" above.) Tool the vertical joints first, then the horizontal joints. Finish by brushing the joints lightly with a whisk broom or soft-bristle brush.

12

Brick Walls

Building a Double-Wythe Wall

The procedures for laying a double-wythe wall are similar to those for a single-wythe wall, except that you'll be laying each course two bricks wide and tying the wythes together, either with header bricks, masonry ties, or a combination of these.

WALL LAYOUT

Mark the footing to locate the outside and inside edges of the wall. For straight walls with no corners, lay a dry course of spaced bricks. In most cases, space the wythes so that the cap bricks will overhang each side of the wall by about ¼ inch. Mark the brick locations, remove them from the foundation, and lay a mortar bed. The bed should be long enough for three bricks, and should be narrower than the wall by ½ inch on each side.

Lay End Bricks. Place and level an end brick for each wythe. Swipe mortar on the ends of two bricks and set them next to the end bricks. Continue laying bricks until you have a base two bricks wide by three bricks long. Check to make sure the bricks are level and aligned. **1** Repeat this procedure at the other end of the wall. Run a string from the end bricks to check whether the ends are level with each other. Build up the mortar bed under one end if necessary; then fill in the rest of the course.

Start a Corner. For walls with corners, lay the wythes and mark their locations. Then lay down two mortar beds about 2 feet long just inside the chalk lines. Lay the first brick on the outer corner; then swipe a ¾-inch layer of mortar on the end of another brick, and lay it at right angles to the first brick. Use a framing square to make sure the corner is square. **2** Adjust as necessary. Then lay two more bricks in each direction. Check frequently with a level and square to make sure the bricks are level and aligned to form a 90-degree angle. Form the backup wythe in the same manner.

Build the Leads. At ends or corners, build leads up to a height of five courses. **3** As you build the leads, lay metal reinforcing ties in the mortar bed at regular intervals (as required by code) to tie the wythes together. The ties should be about 1 inch shorter than the wall width so that the tie ends don't protrude. Check constantly for plumb, level, and square. Use a story pole to ensure consistent course heights. Corner leads will affect construction of end leads.

Fill in Between the Leads. Attach line blocks and string at the top of the lowest course. Fill in the course, working from both leads toward the middle. Rather than filling in all the bricks for one wythe and then moving to the other, lay both wythes as you move down the course. **4** Check frequently with a level to make sure that the wythes are level with each other. After filling in two or three courses, fill the cavity between the wythes with mortar or grout, if required. If the wall will be taller than the initial lead, continue to build up the lead, keeping it three courses higher than the stretcher courses. Complete each course with a closure brick.

When the mortar will hold a thumb-print, clean up and tool the joints.

Cap the Wall. If the wythes are separated only by a ½-inch mortar joint, a cap is optional. A cavity wall, however, requires a cap to keep water out of the wall. The wall may be capped with header bricks placed flat across the width of the wall. For a stronger cap, use rowlock headers laid on edge, as shown. Precast concrete coping is also available. It's usually best to begin with a trial run. Lay all of the bricks dry, with the proper space for mortar joints between them. If the last brick overhangs the end of the wall by more than ¼ inch, adjust the joint spacing or else mark the brick; score it; and cut it. **5** Place metal flashing in the bed joint between the top course and cap bricks for additional moisture protection. Trowel out a mortar bed that covers the wythes and wall cavity. Apply mortar to each brick. For a finished appearance, hide the cut brick four or five bricks in from the end of the wall.

Building a Double-Wythe Wall

TOOLS

- Work gloves
- String and stakes
- Tools for mixing mortar
- Trowels
- Levels
- Hammer and cold chisel
- Striking tool

MATERIALS

- Concrete for footing
- Mortar
- Brick

1 *Start with a dry layout;* then spread mortar and place three bricks in each wythe. Check alignment.

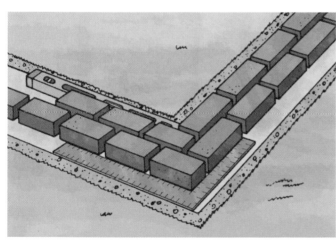

2 *If the wall turns a corner,* use a framing square to make sure the corner is square.

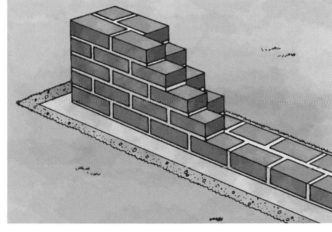

3 *After laying the first course,* build up the ends, or leads, to a height of up to five bricks.

4 *As you work* down the length of the wall, place bricks in each wythe.

5 *If a cap brick* overhangs the wall, either adjust the joint space or score and cut one of the bricks.

12

Brick Walls

CHAPTER 13

Retaining Walls

Basic Requirements

Landscape-Tie Retaining Walls

Interlocking Concrete-Block Walls

Dry-Laid Stone Retaining Walls

Retaining walls prevent soil at a higher grade from tumbling down or eroding to a lower grade. Retaining walls can transform a slope into a series of terraces for lawns, planting beds, or patio areas. On flat sites, low retaining walls can create raised planting beds or borders, adding a sense of visual depth to the landscape.

Basic Requirements

You can make retaining walls from a variety of materials: timber, stone, brick, and concrete block among them. Perhaps the easiest materials for the do-it-yourselfer to work with are mortarless interlocking concrete blocks designed especially for retaining walls. These blocks are discussed in "Interlocking Block Walls," page 202. Timber retaining walls are also easy to build.

No matter which material you choose, retaining walls must be strong enough to hold the weight of the soil placed against them. And you must make provisions for drainage. With tall retaining walls, structural and drainage issues become critical, so it's best to leave the design and construction of tall walls to professionals. Retaining walls smaller than 3 feet high may be designed and built by the do-it-yourselfer, but check with the local building department.

EXCAVATION

The type of excavation required to install the wall depends on wall height, the angle of the slope, and the amount of flat space you wish to create on the downhill side of the wall. On sloped ground, you'll generally cut and fill to create a flat area bounded by a low retaining wall. In the cut-and-fill process, you remove the soil downhill from the proposed wall. If you're building a single retaining wall, it's easiest to cart the soil just downhill and fill in the slope with it. Fill the excavated area behind the wall with tamped sand or gravel to facilitate drainage, and top it off with a layer of topsoil. If you're building a series of terraces and walls, it's easiest to dump the soil into a pile uphill. Fill the area immediately behind the wall as before. Level off the slope from the pile.

Equipment. You can excavate low, short walls with a shovel, pick, and wheelbarrow. Heavy equipment, such as bulldozers, backhoes, and front-end loaders, may be required for larger projects. Unless you know how to operate such equipment, leave the job to an excavation contractor. Even for low walls, you'll need to move a lot of soil, so consider hiring a few strong backs to help with the shovel work.

DRAINAGE

Because wet soil exerts considerable force on a retaining wall, build a drainage system into the wall. Typically, you backfill the wall with gravel; lay perforated pipe; and build weep holes into the wall. The gravel drains water away from the wall, and the drainpipe carries water away from the wall footing. Line the excavation with permeable landscape fabric to keep the gravel from clogging with silt. When planning a drainage system, make sure that you're not directing the water runoff into a neighbor's yard.

Above *Interlocking concrete blocks are stacked one on top of the other; mortar is not used in the installation.*

Weep holes allow subsurface water to drain through the wall. For brick and block walls, you can make weep holes by omitting the mortar from some of the vertical (head) joints near the wall base. Or you can insert 1- or 2-inch diameter PVC pipes in the head joints every 4 to 6 feet along the base of the wall as you build it. If you are building a timber wall, the pipes can be inserted in holes drilled in the wood. In all cases, cover the back of the hole with landscape fabric or fine galvanized wire mesh to help prevent clogging.

Dry-laid retaining walls of stone or interlocking blocks usually require no weep holes because there's no mortar between joints to block drainage.

FOOTINGS AND REINFORCEMENT

Most retaining walls require large, sturdy footings for support. Specific requirements for footings depend on soil conditions, the size and type of wall you're building, and local building codes. Generally, the width of the footing should be at least two-thirds the total wall height. The top of the footing should be at least 12 inches below grade on the downhill side of the wall. The footing should be as thick as the wall width or a minimum of 8 inches. All dimensions may vary, depending on local building codes.

Mortared masonry retaining walls generally have poured-concrete footings with steel reinforcement (rebar) running the length of the footing. Separate rebar extends vertically up into the wall to tie it to the footing. Generally, more of the footing extends behind the wall (uphill side) than in front of it, allowing the weight of

Above *Retaining walls made from landscape timbers have a natural look that tends to blend in with the rest of the yard.*

DRAINAGE SYSTEMS

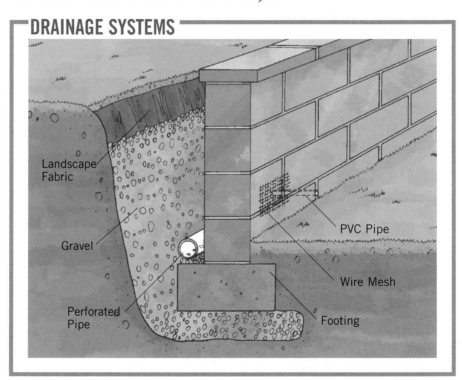

Landscape Fabric

Gravel

Perforated Pipe

PVC Pipe

Wire Mesh

Footing

the soil to keep the wall and footing from tilting forward. The exact orientation of the wall on the footing depends on code and specific site requirements.

Dry-laid stone retaining walls generally don't require poured-concrete footings or reinforcement. Large stones at the base of the wall serve as footings, and planting the crevices between the stones with ground covers or vines helps stabilize the wall and prevents soil erosion.

Landscape-Tie Retaining Walls

Many retaining walls are made from pressure-treated landscape ties. These walls are easy to build and require no footings. Instead, timbers called deadmen are connected at right angles to the wall and extend into the bank behind it to provide additional stability.

BUILDING A LANDSCAPE-TIE WALL

This wall is made of landscape timbers stacked on top of one another and tied together with lengths of ¾-inch rebar. To help resist the tremendous pressure of the soil against the wall, you install timbers (called deadmen) that reach back into the hillside. The deadmen should be a minimum of 3 feet long and are cut from the same size timber as the rest of the wall.

This design works for walls up to 3 feet tall. Walls between 3 and 4 feet need additional reinforcement, and may require a concrete footing. Most codes require any wall over 4 feet tall to be designed by an engineer.

Excavate the Site. Lay out the wall with stakes and string; then excavate a flat area behind it, allowing you room to work. Next, dig a trench approximately 12 inches deep by 16 inches wide along the length of the wall, and backfill it with 6 inches of firmly tamped gravel. In cold climates, extend the bottom of the trench below the frost line.

Lay the First Course. The top edge of the first timber should be at ground level. Lay the first timbers end to end in the trench. Level each timber front to back and side to side using a level as a guide. **1**

Lay Drainage Pipe. Water buildup behind the wall can exert considerable pressure and eventually push timbers forward. A 4-inch-diameter perforated drainpipe behind the wall helps drain it once the wall is constructed. Lay landscape fabric behind the wall, and run it up the hill for about 6 feet. You will use it later as a barrier between the gravel and the topsoil. Lay the pipe (holes down) tight against the wall. **2** If necessary, shovel gravel underneath to slope it about ¼ inch per foot toward one end of the wall. Run the pipe a few inches past the end of the wall to a point where it can exit the ground.

Each course must be set back ¼ inch from the one below it. **3** This helps counteract the weight of the hill against the wall. Lay the second course over the first beginning at the end with a timber cut to half its original length. This strengthens the wall by staggering the joints so that no joint is directly above another. Leave a small space between the ends of adjoining timbers, which will help drain the wall. Spike the courses together with 12-inch galvanized spikes placed about 2 feet from each joint in the upper course.

Install the Deadmen. Align the joints in this course with the joints in the first course. Spike the courses together, as before. Now lay out the deadmen atop the third course so they will fall 4 feet from the wall ends and roughly every 8 feet

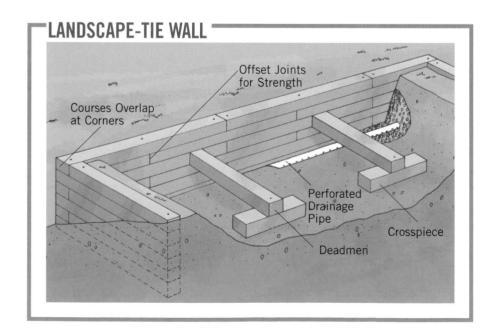

LANDSCAPE-TIE WALL

Offset Joints for Strength

Courses Overlap at Corners

Perforated Drainage Pipe

Crosspiece

Deadmen

Landscape-Tie Retaining Wall

TOOLS

- Shovels and wheelbarrow
- Tamper
- Work gloves and safety glasses
- ¾-in drill
- ¾-in auger bit
- Sledge hammer

MATERIALS

- Treated landscape ties
- Galvanized spikes
- Gravel
- Perforated drainage pipes
- Landscape fabric
- #6 Rebar

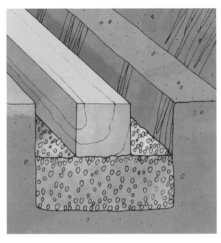

1 *Lay the first timber* on top of at least 6 in. of gravel.

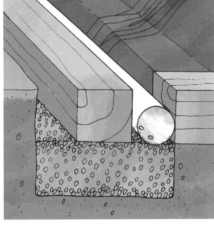

2 *Use PVC drainage* pipe to direct water away.

3 *Set rows* back from the one below it; overlap corners.

4 *Install deadmen;* spike crosspiece into the ground.

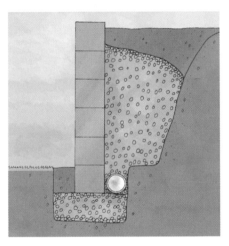

5 *Add gravel;* cover with landscape fabric and topsoil.

between. **4** Spike a 3-foot crosspiece to the end, as shown.

Add Remaining Courses. Cut timbers to fit between the deadmen. Spike this course to the one below it with 12-inch galvanized spikes.

Once all the timbers are in place, drill ¾-inch-diameter holes for the rebar pins that tie the wall together. Drill holes about 8 to 10 inches on either side of the joints in the top of the wall, and continue until they go through the wall and exit the bottom timber. Also drill a hole that goes down through each deadman and into the ground. At the other end of the deadmen, drill holes a few

inches from the end of each crosspiece. Add extensions to the bit when the bit will reach no further.

Drive 24-inch lengths of #6 (¾-inch) rebar pins through the deadman crosspiece and into the ground. Cut the rest of the pins from #6 rebar so that they're 24 inches longer than the wall is high. With a sledgehammer, drive the pins through the timbers into the ground.

Cover the perforated drainpipe with 6-inch layers of tamped gravel up to within 6 inches of the top of the wall; then cover it with the landscape fabric you laid earlier. Complete the fill with topsoil. **5**

Interlocking Concrete-Block Walls

There are many interlocking-block retaining-wall systems on the market. These are available from most patio suppliers, masonry suppliers, major home centers, and other retail sources. The individual blocks are cast to look like natural stone and come in a variety of shapes, colors, and surface textures.

Although installation techniques vary for each brand, most interlock by means of pins, clips, or joints cast into the block itself. No mortar or reinforcing bar is required. Once you provide the required footing (for most manufacturers, a compacted sand or gravel base), you simply lay up the blocks, using the appropriate pins or other fasteners to lock them together.

On most types, the blocks interlock so that each horizontal course is stepped back slightly from the one beneath to create a batter angle.

Prepare the Foundation. Cut and fill for the wall, and lay out the wall with stakes and strings. Excavate a trench along the planned wall location, and compact the soil in the trench bottom. **1** Add a 3- to 6-inch layer of

Interlocking Block Walls

TOOLS

- Work gloves and safety glasses
- Shovel and wheelbarrow
- Soil tamper
- Caulking gun
- Spirit level
- Hammer and brick set
- Circular saw with masonry blade (optional)
- String and mason's blocks

MATERIALS

- Retaining wall block
- Block connectors
- Perforated drainage pipe
- Gravel
- Adhesive for cap block (if necessary)

1 *Dig the trench,* and tamp the soil level at the bottom of the trench.

4 *Place the PVC* pipe behind the first row of blocks. The pipe should rest on gravel and slope slightly.

5 *Place the second course,* staggering the joints to create a running bond pattern.

sand or pea gravel to level the trench and to provide drainage. **2** The total depth of the trench will depend on how much of the wall must extend below grade on the downhill side.

Install the Base Course. Set up stakes and a level string to represent the top front edge of the base course. Lay a row of blocks, orienting them so that the next course can interlock with the base course. The manufacturer's instructions will indicate how to place the blocks so that they'll interlock. As you lay each block, check it for level in both directions. **3** Backfill behind the first course with tamped sand or gravel.

Lay the Drainpipe. Install the drainage pipe on gravel behind the first course of blocks. Grade the gravel so that the pipe slopes slightly to drain water away from the wall. **4**

In the first-course blocks, install any pins or clips, following the manufacturer's assembly instructions. Then fit the second course over the first, staggering the joints to create a running-bond pattern. **5** Backfill behind the second course, covering the drainage pipe with gravel. **6** Cut blocks with a hammer and brick set **7** or a circular saw with masonry blade. Repeat the procedure for each additional course of the wall.

2 **Add 3 to 6 in. of gravel.** Tamp the gravel to provide a level base for the wall.

3 **Lay the first row of blocks.** As you work, check to be sure that each block is level.

6 **With the second** course in place, backfill with gravel to cover the pipe.

7 **To cut the blocks,** score the blocks and use a hammer and brickset or a masonry blade.

(Continued on page 204)

Finish the Wall. Installation requirements may vary. This product uses plastic pegs to help align each course of blocks. **8** It is also necessary to install pegs horizontally between blocks to tie the wall together. **9** Remember some products have each course step back from the one below. **10**

All manufacturers produce matching cap blocks for their walls, but not all walls require a cap. If your wall doesn't require a cap, fill the cores of the top course with gravel or soil, and allow plants to cover the top of the wall. If a cap is recommended, install the blocks with pins, clips, or a special high-strength adhesive recommended by the manufacturer. **11**

smart tip

KEEPING DRAINAGE FLOWING
Perforated PVC pipe is a great way to provide drainage behind a retaining wall. In most installations, you set the pipe on a bed of gravel and then cover with additional gravel. A good precaution to take is to wrap the pipe in a filter fabric. This will keep silt from clogging the pipe.

Interlocking Block Walls (Continued from page 203)

8 *Follow manufacturer's instructions. This product uses plastic pegs to help align the courses.*

9 *Pegs installed horizontally add strength by helping to tie the length of the wall together.*

10 *Check for level and plumb frequently. Most wall systems have a built-in batter.*

11 *Install cap blocks for a finished appearance. This product requires use of an adhesive.*

Dry-Laid Stone Retaining Walls

Dry-laid stones create a natural-looking retaining wall. Construction is similar to building a dry-laid freestanding wall, although the retaining wall usually requires a wider base and a greater batter angle. (See "Dry-Laid Stone Walls," page 132.) Generally, the width of the wall at the base should equal at least half the wall height. In most situations, large base stones serve as the wall footing, so no poured-concrete footing is needed. As with freestanding walls, you must pay careful attention to selecting and fitting the stones.

Depending on the size and shape of your stones, and the wall height, you can build the wall one, two, or even three wythes thick. Lay two stones over one and one stone over two. Use bond stones to tie the wythes together every 4 to 6 feet and at each end of the wall. Ideally, some of these stones should extend behind the wall so that the weight of the earth will hold them in place. The largest, flattest stones are used for the base. It's best to leave the construction of stone retaining walls more than 3 feet tall to experienced stonemasons.

BUILDING A DRY-LAID RETAINING WALL

Excavate the site. Cut and fill to create a space for the wall. Lay out the wall with stakes and strings, and excavate a level trench about twice as wide as the proposed bottom course of stones. Dig the trench deep enough to house the base stones. In wet or unstable soils, dig a deeper trench and add 2 to 3 inches of compacted sand or gravel to promote drainage. Line the cutout area with landscape fabric to keep the gravel you'll put there from clogging.

Select the largest and flattest stones for the base course. Lay them in the trench so that they tilt slightly toward the bank. Use large, flat bond stones at each end of the wall and at 4- to 6-foot intervals along it. Between the bond stones, lay stones one in front of the other to create a double-wythe wall. Long bond stones can extend behind the back of the wall and be cut into the bank to help support the wall. After laying the first course, replace any soil on the front side of the wall, and tamp firmly. Install a perforated drainpipe behind the wall.

Add the Backfill. Place the next course of stones set back slightly from the first course to start the batter angle. Continue to add bond stones, which extend back toward the hillside. To prevent the stones from toppling, begin filling the uphill side of the wall with gravel. Add enough fill to bring the gravel to the same level as the top of the highest stones; then tamp it.

Add Remaining Courses. Build up the remaining courses, stepping the stones slightly back against the slope, staggering joints, and installing bond stones periodically. Fill the gaps between large stones with small rubble stones. Use a batter gauge so that you can be sure that the wall angles back 1 to 2 inches per 1 foot of height. Continue backfilling with gravel: every time you complete one or two courses, add gravel up to the top of the wall, and tamp it. Add another one or two courses; then backfill, and so on. Backfill to within 4 inches of the top of the wall, and cover with topsoil.

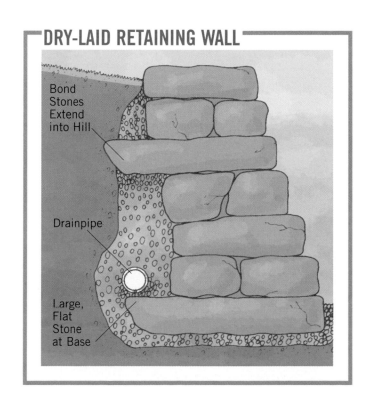

DRY-LAID RETAINING WALL

Bond Stones Extend into Hill

Drainpipe

Large, Flat Stone at Base

Designing and Building
Patios

Gallery of Patio

1 Natural stone patios look best when placed in a natural, rustic setting. Note how the stone path leads the eye into the garden.

2 Concrete is a good, all-purpose patio material, especially in areas that will get a lot of use, such as this pool setting.

3 Let the surroundings dictate the type of material you use on your patio. Here local stone works well with the shingled house.

4 Ceramic tile adds a distinctive look to any outdoor setting. Be sure the tiles you select are designed for exterior use.

5 Interlocking concrete pavers are manufactured products that come in a variety of
styles and colors. Here they are made to
look like brick pavers. This type of product
is usually installed over a sand base.

6 The designer of this patio got a helping hand
from nature. The spaces between the stones
are filled by a flowering ground cover.

7 Slate takes on different looks depending on
how it is installed. These random sizes
placed over a sand base have an informal
appearance. Using all similar sizes and
attaching them to a mortar base would
make the area appear more formal.

Designs

Gallery of Patio Designs

6

1 Depending on the thickness of the material, brick pavers can be installed on either a sand or mortar base.

2 Select patio materials based on how the area will be used. For example, the area around a pool, hot tub, or spa should be one that is not slippery when wet.

3 You can soften the look of any patio, even this grid of tiles, by allowing border plants to spill over the edges of the patio. Groupings of container plants also help.

4 As with walkways, patios can be created using loose material, such as river-washed stone.

5 Details can make the difference in your patio design. Here colorful accent tiles add a little visual punch to this tile-covered patio.

6 When planning a patio, remember that they are always part of a larger area. The open design of this patio does not take away from the surrounding view.

CHAPTER 14

Soft-Set Patios

Types of Patios

Installing Patio Pavers

A well-designed patio is likely to add more to the value of your home than it costs to build. Patios can be anything from a simple small pad outside the back door to a large expanse wrapping around a corner of the house. Typically, however, a patio is about one-third the size of the house—larger perhaps than any room in the home. A 1,500-square-foot house, for example, might sport a 500-square-foot patio, one perhaps measuring 20 by 25 feet.

Site your patio to protect it from the hottest sun and coldest wind. Moreover, consider the terrain. You want your patio in an area that is well drained, and at the same time, you want to make sure you're not blocking or disrupting the existing drainage. To keep it from flooding, a

patio is usually built an inch or so above ground level. To keep rain and melting snow from leaking inside, the patio should slope away from the house at a rate of ¼ inch per foot and should meet it 1 to 3 inches below the floor of the house.

Types of Patios

Patios are much like walks, in that you can lay them over one of two kinds of bases. The simplest is a sand-and-gravel base, which will support flagstone, brick, or interlocking pavers. Mortared brick and stone patios, on the other hand, sit in a mortar bed on top of a concrete pad laid slightly below grade.

The easiest patio you can build uses concrete pavers, brick, flagstone, or adobe block laid on a sand-and-gravel subbase. Pavers and flagstone of various sizes, shapes, colors, and textures come

in a variety of patterns, but anything thinner than 1¼ inches may crack with use. The secret of success in dry-laid paving is a proper subbase, which minimizes settlement. The subbase consists of a 4-inch layer of gravel, topped off with an easy-to-smooth sand layer. On poorly drained soils and in very cold climates, the drainage base should be 6 inches thick. In some soils and in areas where the ground does not freeze and thaw, you may be able to do without the gravel entirely. Check with your local building office.

Edging. Edging holds the patio surface in place and keeps the individual pavers from moving. If the patio is built at ground level, the earth can serve as an edging. But to discourage flooding, you may want to build your patio slightly higher than grade and put an edging around it. You have your choice of picking an edging that blends with the patio or one that complements the patio material.

Opposite left *There are a variety of patio materials available, but perhaps the most straightforward type, and an easy one to build, consists of bricks on a tamped-sand base.*

Above left *If your patio will be close to your house, try to limit the size of the outdoor area to one-third the size of the house.*

Above *Place your patio so that it takes the best advantage of the local climate.*

smart tip

EDGING OPTIONS
The simplest type of edging is rot-resistant or pressure-treated wood. A harder-to-install but attractive edging uses pavers set on edge or on end in surrounding trenches. The pavers hold best if they're laid in mortar.

Left Small patios placed within gardens offer a stopping-off spot that allows someone walking through the yard to stop and admire the surrounding area.

Installing Patio Pavers

Concrete pavers, available at home-improvement centers, can be used to make a simple, attractive patio. Pavers usually have a tab system that helps you space the blocks accurately without measuring. Concrete pavers are available in a variety of patterns, and installation will vary slightly from brand to brand and pattern to pattern. All concrete paving blocks, however, can be laid over a sand-and-gravel bed. The basic principles for building a paver patio are given below, but be sure to follow the manufacturer's directions as well.

Lay Out the Patio. Use wood 1x2 stakes and string lines to outline your patio. Begin by driving two stakes near the house wall at the patio edges. Set up batter boards at the outer corners. Stretch mason's twine along what will be the perimeter of your patio. (Mason's twine stretches less than string.) Level the twine by hanging a line level at midspan.

Check to make sure the layout is square using the 3-4-5 triangle method. Measure from one stake 3 feet along the house, then 4 feet along the line. The corner is square if the diagonal between the two points measures 5 feet. If the corner is not square, slide the string along the batter boards until it is, and mark the location of the string on the board. For large areas, increase the measurements proportionally. For example, increase the measurements to 6, 8, and 10 feet.

Square the second line that meets the house; then square the remaining side of the patio.

When all the sides are placed properly, make a saw cut where each string line crosses its batter board. If you need to remove the strings during subsequent work, you can pop them back in the cuts without having to remeasure.

Plot the Slope. To drain well, the patio should slope away from the house ¼ inch per foot. Adjust your level string lines to reflect this. If, for example, the patio is 12 feet wide, the edge nearest the house needs to be 3 inches higher than the far end (12 feet times ¼ inch per foot equals 3 inches). In this case, you would slide the string 3 inches up the stake nearest the house. Compute the slope for your patio, and mark the new location with a saw cut. Slide the string up into the cut.

Sprinkle sand or flour over the strings to transfer the layout to the ground. Where the strings cross to mark the corner of the patio, suspend a plumb bob from the line, and mark the corner with a nail struck through a piece of paper into the ground.

Determine Depth. Begin by digging out the sod and all organic material. Then dig deep enough to allow for the depth of the pavers, plus a 1½-inch sand subbase, plus 4 to 6 inches of gravel. (Check with your local building department to find out the required depth.) To determine the depth of the excavation, first figure out the total thickness of the finished patio. If the pavers sit on 1½ inches of sand, for example, and the required gravel subbase is 4 inches, the combined thickness is 7 inches (1½+1½+4=7). If you wanted to have the surface 1 inch above grade, the depth of the excavation at the end farthest from the house would be 6 inches—7 inches for the patio thickness minus 1 inch for the elevation. In this case, you dig a hole 6 inches deep at the batter boards. To slope the bed, measure from the bottom of the string to the bottom of the hole. Keep the bottom of the excavation

roughly this distance from the string.

Compact the soil by tamping and leveling it. **1** Some masons like to cover the bare earth with a landscape fabric to discourage weed growth.

Lay the Gravel Base. Lay a 4- to 6-inch layer of gravel as required by code. Spread the gravel about 1 foot beyond the edges of the patio on all sides. Tamp the gravel down. **2** For large spaces, rent a mechanical tamper.

Roll landscape fabric out over the tamped gravel. **3** Overlap the fabric at least 6 inches at the seams. The fabric prevents the sand from infiltrating the gravel.

14

Soft-Set Patios

Patio Pavers on a Sand Base

TOOLS	MATERIALS
▨ Work gloves	▨ Gravel
▨ Safety glasses	▨ Sand
▨ String	▨ Pavers
▨ Line level	▨ Edging material
▨ 4-ft. level	
▨ Tamper	
▨ 1½-in.-diameter pipe	
▨ Mallet	
▨ Screed board	
▨ Stiff-bristled broom	

1 *Excavate the area* to the desired depth. Tamp down and level the soil.

2 *Add a 4- to 6-in. layer* of gravel. Tamp the gravel using a hand or mechanical tamper.

3 *Spread landscape fabric* over the gravel. Overlap seams by at least 6 in.

(Continued on page 218)

Place the Edging. If you removed the strings in the course of placing the gravel, retie them. Dig a deeper trench around the perimeter of the excavation, as needed, to hold the edging. Measure down from the layout lines periodically to make sure the trench will put your edging at the desired height—at or just below the finished elevation of the pavers.

Install edging on two sides—one of which should be the house wall. Set the edging flush with or slightly below what will be the surface of the patio. **4**

Spread a thin layer of fine sand over the gravel base to keep the coarser sand from chok-ing the gravel. Then spread a coarse concrete sand over the gravel to create a layer 1½ inches deep. **5** To level the bed, place pipes with a 1½-inch outer diameter along the edges of the patio. Push the pipes down into the sand until the top of the pipe is at the proper grade, as measured from the strings. Level the sand by laying a 2x4 across the pipes and sliding it along the pipes. **6** Remove the pipes when you're done.

Lay the Pavers. Starting in a corner, begin laying pavers on the smooth sand. Tap each one several times with a rubber mallet to set it

Patio Pavers on a Sand Base

4 **Install the edging.** *This system uses a plastic edging, but bricks set on edge is an option.*

5 **Shovel the sand** *over the landscape fabric. Try to get the sand as smooth as possible.*

8 **To trim small pavers,** *clamp the paver to a worktable and cut with a masonry blade.*

9 **Go back over the patio** *with a mallet and 2x4 to make sure the pavers are seated properly.*

firmly on the sand. **7** Avoid twisting the units into place, as that disturbs the sand subbase. The exact order in which you lay the blocks will depend on the pattern of the patio.

Most block pavers have built-in spacers to create a minimum joint width. If you're working with ones that don't, space them to create ¹⁄₁₆- to ⅛-inch joints.

To cut a small paver, clamp it to a worktable and cut with a carbide masonry blade. **8** If your work requires you to stand or kneel in the subbase, lay down a sheet of plywood to keep from disturbing the smooth sand. Continue setting the rest of the pavers. **9**

Complete the Edging. If you're working with rectangular pavers, install the outer edging snugly against the pavers. If you're working with irregular units, install the edging with space to spare; then cut units to fill the spaces.

Fill the Joints. Complete the patio by sweeping fine, dry mortar sand into the joints between units and around the edges. **10** Spray the surface with a hose to wet down the sand. **11** You may need to repeat sweeping and wetting the sand to completely fill the joints. When you can sweep sand across the patio and end with the same pile you began with, joint-filling is finished.

(Continued from page 217)

6 *Embed 1½-in. pipes* in the sand to use as a guide for your 2x4 screed board.

7 *Begin placing the pavers.* Seat each paver with a tap of a rubber mallet; check for level.

10 *Brush dry* sand into the joints between pavers. Brush in all directions for even coverage.

11 *Wet down the sand* using a fine mist from a garden hose. Don't dislodge the sand.

14

Soft-Set Patios

Mortar-Bed Patios

Concrete Patios

Patios on Concrete Slabs

Above *Use a concrete slab as a base for another material, or smooth it to create a concrete patio.*

This chapter deals with setting permanent patios. You can either pour a concrete patio, where the concrete serves as the finish surface. Concrete forms a hard, even, stonelike surface that requires little maintenance. Reasonably easy to build and long lasting, it's the basic home patio. Or you can cover the concrete with a more decorative patio material, such as brick, stone, or tile.

Concrete Patios

For a small patio—80 square feet or less—you can buy a prepackaged concrete mix and mix it in a wheelbarrow. For a larger patio, you can purchase the separate ingredients—portland cement, sand, and gravel—and mix them yourself. Perhaps the most practical method is to have ready-mix concrete delivered by truck to the job site. Ready-mix is sold by the cubic yard, and every 100 square feet of 4-inch-thick patio requires roughly 1.23 cubic yards. A 450-square-foot patio would require 4.5 x 1.23 cubic yards—just over 5½ cubic yards of ready-mix. Add 10 percent for spillage.

Consider ordering air-entrained mix. Air-entrained concrete contains billions of microscopic air bubbles in the hardened slab that act as safety valves to prevent damage caused by freezing and thawing.

To order ready-mix, call your dealer at least a day ahead of time. Tell him when you want delivery—the day, time, place, and number of cubic yards. Tell the supplier exactly what you're using the concrete for, so you'll get the right mix. Typically, you'll want a mix with

- ¾-inch maximum-size coarse aggregate (stones).
- A minimum of six 94-pound bags of portland cement in each cubic yard—for good finishing.
- A maximum slump of 5 inches for hand methods of finishing—slump is a measure of workability.
- From 5 to 7 percent entrained air by volume in a severe climate, and from 3 to 4½ percent in a nonfreezing climate—to aid in finishing.
- A 28-day compressive strength of at least 4,000 pounds per square inch (psi). Compressive strength is a good measure of the strength and durability you'll have in the hardened concrete; a 3,500-psi compressive strength is sufficient for a nonfreezing climate. Check the local building department for recommendations.

If you order ready-mix this way, it should arrive ready to use without adding any water to make it workable. In fact, you should avoid adding water, as that cuts down on the strength and durability of your patio.

If the truck mixer cannot safely back up and dump into your patio forms, you can have the ready-mix pumped through a hose to the construction site. The hose can be routed through a gate, over a fence, or wherever necessary to reach from street to patio. If you think you'll need to have the concrete pumped to the site, be sure to discuss this with the supplier.

On concreting day have two or more strong helpers on hand when the truck mixer arrives. If the ready-mix will be brought in from the street by wheelbarrow, have an additional two helpers to man the wheelbarrows. Each worker should have work gloves and eye protection. At least one worker—who may have to wade into the mix while placing it—will need rubber boots. Once the concrete is poured, you'll need time to screed (flatten) it and to work the surface several times to create the finish you desire.

MAKING A CONCRETE PATIO

Building a concrete patio is much like building a concrete walk. After excavating the area, spread a 4- to 6-inch gravel base. Once the base is prepared, you set the forms, pour the concrete, and work it with a variety of tools to create the desired surface. Check with the local building department concerning requirements in your area.

Lay out the perimeter of the patio by stretching strings from stakes driven at the house to batter boards at the far end of the patio. Check to make sure the layout is square using the 3-4-5 triangle method. (See "Using the 3-4-5

Method, page 153.) The patio needs to slope ¼ inch per foot for drainage. Set level strings, and adjust to get the proper slope.

Excavate for the Patio. Dig out the sod and all organic material. Dig deep enough to accommodate a slab 4 inches thick plus any required gravel drainage base. Measure down from the string lines to slope the excavation for proper drainage. **1** Dig a few inches beyond the edges of the slab to allow room for the concrete forms. Try to level the bottom of the excavation. Remove large stones with a pry bar. **2** Fill the excavation with any gravel required. **3**

Building a Concrete Patio

TOOLS
- Work gloves
- Tamper
- Rake
- Line level
- Wheelbarrow
- Power drill-driver
- Bull float
- Edging and jointing trowels
- Pry bar (optional)

MATERIALS
- Mason string
- Welded-wire mesh
- Gravel
- Concrete mix
- Burlap
- Lumber for forms

1 *Measure up from the bottom* of the excavation on a stake. Use a string and level to adjust the slope.

2 *Prepare the base* by leveling the area and removing any large rocks with a pry bar.

3 *Add gravel* over the entire patio area, and rake it smooth and even.

15 Mortar-Bed Patios

(Continued on page 224)

Build the Forms. Next, position 2x4 forms around the edge of the patio, cutting them to length as necessary. (See "Building Forms," page 152.) Make sure the stakes supporting the forms don't protrude above the form boards. **4**

You'll be using the forms later to level the patio, so check your work as you go by measuring down from the strings to make sure the forms follow the required slope.

Screed the Gravel. Use a screed to smooth out the gravel as much as possible. The gravel should be about even with the bottom edges of the form boards. **5** Go over the entire patio

with a power tamper to settle the gravel into position. **6**

Add Wire Reinforcement. The concrete must be reinforced with #6 wire reinforcing mesh that has 6x6-inch openings. **7** Place stones or pieces of brick under the wire mesh to raise it about 2 inches above the gravel, so it will fall roughly in the middle of the finished slab.

Place Expansion Strips. If the patio butts against an existing structure, such as a house foundation, steps, or a walk, you must also place an expansion strip between the patio and

Building a Concrete Patio

4 *Build 2x4 forms* to hold the concrete; set stakes below the top of the form boards.

5 *Screed the gravel* until it's level. The gravel should be no higher than the bottom of the boards.

8 *Begin the pour;* dump each load against the previous one. Fill to just above the forms.

9 *Screed the concrete.* This begins the leveling process and helps fill in any voids.

the existing structure. (See "Install Expansion Strips," page 107.)

Pour the Concrete. Transport fresh ready-mix as smoothly and gently as possible in a wheelbarrow with pneumatic tires to keep the ingredients from separating. **8** Don't dump and drag concrete into place, as that separates the ingredients. Overfill the forms slightly.

Remove Air Bubbles. During the pour, remove air bubbles by moving a shovel up and down through the pour. This is especially important near the edges and corners.

Screed the Surface. Start finishing the patio by screeding the surface to make it flat. **9** Use a 2x4 that's 1 or 2 feet longer than the distance between forms as the screed. If necessary, have a partner work from one side of the pour while you work from the other. Screed the surface twice.

Float the Surface Smooth. Immediately give the fresh slab a preliminary surfacing using either a darby or a bull float. **10** This pushes aggregate below the surface and begins the leveling process. (See "Finishing the Concrete Surface," page 108.) To create a slip-resistant surface, go over the concrete with a broom. **11**

(Continued from page 223)

6 *Tamp the gravel. Using a power tamper will make the work go quicker.*

7 *Cover the entire slab area with wire reinforcing mesh. Overlap seams by at least 6 in.*

10 *Using a darby or bull float, push the aggregate below the surface.*

11 *Give the surface some "tooth" by going over the uncured slab with a broom.*

15

Mortar-Bed Patios

(Continued on page 226)

Avoid overworking the concrete, as that makes the surface less durable. Work until water begins to form on the surface of the pour. The water brings a fine coat of sand and cement with it, and too much will weaken the top layer of the pour.

Edge the Pad. The edge of a concrete pad should be rounded over slightly to keep it from chipping during normal wear. The task is done with a tool called an edger. Put the blade of the edger in the space between the pad and the forms, and rest the surface of the edger on the pad. **12** Move the edger back and forth, with the leading edge raised to prevent gouging. (Some edgers have a rolled up leading edge and don't need to be lifted.)

Cut the Control Joints. Control joints are the grooves you see on sidewalks roughly every 3 feet. They're designed to control cracking as the slab hardens and are cut with a jointing tool. Get one with a ½-inch radius cutter that is 1 inch deep. Guide the tool along a straight board that rests on the forms and stretches across the pad. **13** (This isn't necessary if you are covering the slab with another material.)

Control jointing should divide the patio into

A Concrete Patio (Continued from page 225)

12 *To create a stronger edge,* run an edging tool along the perimeter of the pour.

13 *A jointing tool* is used to create control joints in the slab. Control joints prevent cracking.

14 *Mist the surface,* and cover with burlap or polyethylene sheeting.

15 *Cure the slab* for at least 5 to 7 days. Mist the surface periodically.

panels no larger than 8 feet on each side. A 16-by 24-foot patio, for example, would be jointed into six panels with one control joint 8 feet from the longer edge and a control joint 8 feet from each of the shorter edges. To be effective, control joints must be at least one-fourth the slab thickness—1 inch deep on a patio slab. Mark the forms to show where the joints will meet the edge of your patio.

Float the Surface. Wait until the water sheen has left the surface of the concrete. Test the surface by standing on it. If your foot leaves a depression of no more than ¼ inch, the concrete is ready for a final floating.

The best hand float to use—especially for air-entrained concrete—is a magnesium float. Float by moving the tool flat against the surface in sweeping arcs, adding a slight sawing motion. Cut off any bumps; fill holes; and level the ridges as you go. Work from the edges first; then use a pair of knee boards to get out onto the slab.

If you stop working the surface at this point, it is likely to be rough and uneven. Edge, joint, and float a second time. This not only makes the surface smoother, it further compresses the concrete at the surface, making it stronger and more durable.

Let the Pad Cure. To gain maximum strength and durability, your concrete patio should be cured for five to seven days—the longer the better. The most practical methods of curing are by spraying on a curing compound or by spreading 6-mil polyethylene sheeting or burlap over the slab and weighing it down with sand. **14** If you are using burlap, spray it with water periodically over the next few days. **15** Do not use curing compound on a slab that is to be covered with bricks or stones.

smart tip

RAISING THE SLAB
To raise a slab or to correct one with the wrong slope, apply a mortar bed made of portland cement and sand mixed 1:5. This method is useful for bridging irregularities or when you need to reshape a surface to improve drainage.

Patterned Concrete Systems

Although not a do-it-yourself project, patterned concrete (some companies refer to the process as stamping, stenciling, or texturing) provides a good way to get the look of natural stone or brick while using concrete. Some samples are shown here, but for a wider selection, check the manufacturers in the resource guide.

15

Mortar-Bed Patios

Left Flagstone makes an attractive mortared patio. **Above** Brick pavers with crisp mortar joints is a classic patio combination.

Patios on Concrete Slabs

The most elegant-looking patios are made of flagstone, brick, or tile, and are mortared together. These patios wear and weather well, and are quite durable. Like mortared walks, mortared patios sit on a concrete slab to provide support and prevent cracking. Pouring a slab and applying the brick, stone, or tile is a serious time commitment. You can often shortcut the process by applying stone or brick over an existing concrete patio.

If you'd like to build a stone or brick patio from the ground up, pour a slab as described in "Making a Concrete Patio," page 223. Dig and lay the base so that pad elevation will place the pavers at the desired height. Then follow the directions below.

Covering an Existing Concrete Patio. The concrete base slab may be new or old, but it must be clean, sound, and free of oil, grease, and loose materials such as dust, paint, and efflorescence. Clean the slab thoroughly with a solution of 1 part muriatic acid to 9 parts water. This is a strong acid: for safety's sake, pour the water first, then the acid. Wear heavy rubber gloves, long sleeves, goggles, and a vapor respirator. Apply the solution with a stiff-bristle brush. Rinse thoroughly with clean water.

A scaled surface that is structurally sound presents no problem because the new surface will cover it. If the slab has settled unevenly, in most cases it can be corrected by installing the units on a thick, corrective layer of mortar. Every crack and joint in the old slab, however, must coincide with a joint in the new paving. Otherwise, movement across the crack or joint will damage the new paving.

Cover all joints and cracks in the base slab with something to hold the mortar—½- by ½-inch sticky-back weather stripping will work. Follow the cracks faithfully.

Paving raises the elevation of a slab—make sure you have room for what you're planning. It wouldn't do to have your patio end up higher than the house floor, for example. In fact, to prevent flooding, make sure that there is at least a 1-inch drop from the threshold to the new patio surface.

FLAGSTONE AND BRICK PATIOS

Both flagstone and brick make excellent finish patio materials. Once you have prepared the slab, install these materials as you would for a mortared-bed walks as described in "Finishing the Walk," page 110.

TILING A PATIO

Ceramic patio tiles create a formal look unlike any other tiling material. Tiles used outdoors not only must be low in water absorption to resist damage from freezing and thawing but should have a surface that does not get slippery when wet. It is vital that the tile you select be approved by its manufacturer for outdoor use.

In tile work, the tiles are set in a thin-set mortar adhesive that is combed with a notched trowel, and the joints are filled with grout. The two materials are very similar.

Existing Slabs. If you're using an existing slab, it should be structurally sound and free of oil and waxy films and foreign matter. The slab should be properly sloped, well-drained, and suitably flat, and not subject to dampness from beneath. (For drainage problems, see the Smart Tip on page 227.) If the surface has been troweled, be sure to coat it with a concrete bonder.

Begin by snapping layout lines on the con-crete slab. It is best to do a dry run before applying the adhesive. **1**

Spread the Mortar. To tile over a concrete slab following the thin-set method, first dampen the concrete slab. Thin-set mortar should be mixed to a smooth-paste consistency, according to label's instructions. Then use the flat side of a notched trowel to spread mortar out over the slab, aiming for about a ½-inch layer. Comb the mortar with the notched side of the trowel, holding it at a 45-degree angle to the slab. **2** Set the field tiles leaving room for any edge tiles that must be trimmed to fit. **3**

Tiling a Patio

TOOLS

- Tools needed for concrete slab if necessary
- Work gloves
- Notched trowel
- Chalk-line box
- Tile cutters
- Mallet
- Sponge
- Rubber float

MATERIALS

- Tile
- Plastic spacers
- Thin-set adhesive
- Grout
- Plastic sheeting
- Backer rod if necessary
- Tile sealer

1 *Snap chalk lines* on the prepared slab. Lay out the tiles in a dry run; adjust the layout to minimize cuts.

2 *Apply a coat* of the thin-set mortar with a notched trowel, holding the tool at a angle.

3 *Set the field tiles* first. Border tiles should be cut and installed last.

15 **Mortar-Bed Patios**

(Continued on page 230)

Use Spacers. When setting individual ceramic tiles, you must allow space between them for the grout joints. To ensure uniform joints, buy molded plastic spacers from the tile dealer. (See Step 3 on page 229.) These small plastic crosses come in various sizes; ½ inch is the typical space between quarry tiles installed for an outdoor application. Some spacers can be removed (before the adhesive cures) and reused. Others can be left in place and grouted over.

Some tiles have a textured back. To ensure 100 percent mortar coverage with no voids to collect water and freeze, coat the back of such tiles with thinset. You can test the coverage you're getting by pulling off several tiles that are already laid. Before the mortar hardens, level the tiles with a piece of scrap 2x8 and a hammer. Place the scrap on the tiles, and tap gently, pressing the tiles into place.

When the field tiles are set, begin cutting and placing the border tiles. **4** To allow for slight variations in the field, measure and set each border tile separately. **5** Cover the patio area with plastic sheeting, and allow the thinset to cure. **6**

If the patio abuts another structure, install foam backer rod between the two. **7** Fill this joint with an exterior-grade caulk. **8**

Tiling a Patio (Continued from page 229)

4 **Use a snap cutter** or tile saw to cut the border tiles if necessary. Seat tiles using a mallet.

5 **Measure each border** tile separately to compensate for slight variations in the slab or field tiles.

8 **Caulk all perimeter** joints with a high-quality, exterior-grade caulk.

9 **Mix tile grout,** and apply it with a rubber float. Work the grout into the spaces between tiles.

Grout the Joints. Pry out all tile spacers, if necessary. Lightly dampen the tiles, and spread properly mixed commercial tile grout over them. Work diagonally across the tiles, pushing the mortar into the joints with a rubber grout float. **9** Let the grout set for about 15 minutes. Then wipe the tiles clean with a damp sponge. **10** Let them dry for about 40 minutes, until a haze forms and the grout firms. Polish off the haze with a soft, clean cloth.

Keep the area damp and cover with plastic for three to seven days. Apply a clear tile sealer to the surface, following directions on the sealer bottle. **11**

smart tip

PERMANENT FORMS
On large areas that are difficult to level and finish, you can install permanent intermediate forms that will divide the pour into more manageable sections. To attach intermediate boards, make square cuts and screw them to the perimeter forms. Brace the boards with stakes, but recess them below the boards so that they don't interfere with screeding.

15

Mortar-Bed Patios

6 *After setting the tiles,* cover them with plastic sheeting and allow them to cure, usually 24 to 48 hours.

7 *Place foam backer rod* into any opening larger than ¼ in. around the perimeter of the patio.

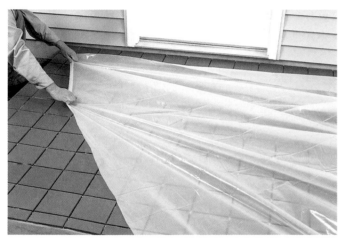

10 *Wipe off the tile haze* with a damp sponge. Be careful not to dislodge any grout.

11 *After the grout cures,* apply a tile sealer. Follow the manufacturer's application schedule.

Resource Guide

The following list of manufacturers and associations is meant to be a general guide to additional industry and product-related sources. It is not intended as a listing of products and manufacturers represented by the photographs in this book.

Acme Brick Company *is a manufacturer that designs bricks for architectural and residential projects. Its Web site provides information and masonry designer service to consumers.*
P. O. Box 425
Fort Worth, TX 76101
Phone: 800-792-1234 ex. 365
www.brick.com

American Institute of Architects (AIA) *offers a Web site with up-to-date news, an event calendar, and other information. The main purpose of the AIA's Web site is to help professionals, but the site does help consumers locate architects.*
1735 New York Ave., NW
Washington, DC 20006-5292
Phone: 800-242-3837
www.aia.org

Anchor Wall Systems *produces a line of interlocking concrete-block wall products. The Web site offers consumer information and project plans.*
5959 Baker Rd., Suite 390
Minnetonka, MN 53345
Phone: 877-295-5415
www.anchorwall.com

Artcrete, Inc., *manufactures faux brick for driveways, paths, and patios.*
5812 Hwy. 494
Natchitoches, LA 71457
Phone: 318-379-2000
www.artcrete.com

Bomanite *is a manufacturer of stamped and imprinted concrete, as well as accessories, sealers, and concrete curing products.*
232 S. Schnoor Ave.
Madera, CA 93637
Phone: 559-673-2411
www.bomanite.com

Boulder Creek Stone Products *manufactures thin brick, floor tile pavers, stone veneer, and accessories.*
8282 Arthur St., NE
Minneapolis, MN 55432
Phone: 800-762-5902
www.bouldercreekstone.com

The Brick Industry Association *promotes manufacturers and distributors interests. Its Web site provides free information to homeowners.*
11490 Commerce Park Dr.
Reston, VA 20191-1525
Phone: 703-620-0010
www.bia.org

Cast Stone Institute *is a nonprofit trade organization that aims to improve the quality of cast stone.*
10 W. Kimball St.
Winder, GA 30680-2535
Phone: 770-868-5909
www.caststone.org

Ceramic Tile Institute of America, Inc. (CTIOA), *supports the expanded use of ceramic tile. Its Web site provides tile information for consumers.*
12061 W. Jefferson Blvd.
Culver City, CA 90230-6219
Phone: 310-574-7800
www.ctioa.org

Concrete Foundations Association of North America *provides educational resources to engineers, contractors, producers, concrete suppliers, and consumers in both U.S. and Canada.*
107 First St. W.
P. O. Box 204
Mount Vernon, IA 52314
Phone: 319-895-6940
www.cfawalls.org

Endicott Clay Products Co. *is a designer of commercial, residential, and landscape brick products.*
P. O. Box 17
Fairbury, NE 68352
Phone: 402-729-3315
www.endicott.com

The Hearth, Patio, and Barbecue Association (HPBA) *promotes the hearth-products industry through information to consumers. Its members include manufacturers, retailers, installation firms, and distributors.*
1601 N. Kent St., Ste. 1001
Arlington, VA 22209
Phone: 703-522-0086
www.hpba.org

Interlocking Concrete Pavement Institute (ICPI) *is a membership organization that educates homeowners, designers, and contractors about different types of concrete paving products that are available.*
1444 I St. NW, Ste. 700
Washington, DC 20005-2210
Phone: 202-712-9036
www.icpi.org

The International Masonry Institute *offers design assistance and information to the public. It also helps consumers find professional craftworkers.*
42 East St.
Annapolis, MD 21401
Phone: 800-464-0988
www.imiweb.org

J & N Stone *produces manufactured stone products, including cobblestone, field pavers, ashlar, and other types of stone.*
13729 David Dr.
Grabill, IN 46741
Phone: 260-627-2404
www.jnstone.com

Keystone Retaining Walls *offers a broad line of retaining wall products, from residential to commercial units.*
4444 W. 78th St.
Minneapolis, MN 55435
Phone: 800-747-8971
www.keystonewalls.com

National Association of Home Builders Research Center *provides information on housing technology.*
400 Prince George's Blvd.
Upper Marlboro, MD 20774
Phone: 800-638-8556
www.nahbrc.org

Portland Cement Association *provides handbooks, resources, and research reports to improve the quality of concrete construction.*
5420 Old Orchard Rd.
Skokie, IL 60077
Phone: 847-966-6200
www.portcement.org

Stone Info.com, *a division of KD Resources, has a Web site that offers valuable information to construction professionals.*
8711 E. Pinnacle Peak Rd.
Scottsdale, AZ 85255
Phone: 480-502-5354
www.stoneinfo.com

Taylor Clay Products *manufactures a wide variety of face bricks in many different colors and shapes in both standard and custom sizes.*
P. O. Box 2128
Salisbury, NC 28145
Phone: 704-636-2411
www.taylorclay.com

Unilock *manufactures products such as standard pavers, textured pavers, and retaining and garden wall blocks.*
Unilock-New York
51 International Blvd.
Brewster, NY 10509
Phone: 800-864-5625
www.unilock.com

Versa-lok Retaining Wall Systems *produces interlocking-block wall systems for residential and commercial uses. The company provides installation tips and landscape ideas.*
6348 Hwy. 36
Oakdale, MN 55128
Phone: 651-770-3166
www.versa-lok.com

Glossary

Actual dimensions The measured dimensions of a masonry unit.

Aggregate Crushed stone, gravel, or other material added to cement to make concrete or mortar. Gravel and crushed stone are considered course aggregate; sand is considered fine aggregate.

Air-entrained concrete Mixture that contains tiny air pockets that allow moisture to freeze and thaw without damaging the structure. Common in cold climates.

Backfill Sand, gravel, pea stone, crushed stone, slag, or cinders used for filling around foundations or piping. In general, to backfill is to replace earth in a trench or around a foundation.

Bat A brick that is cut in half lengthwise.

Bed joint Horizontal masonry joint, opposed to a vertical masonry joint (head joint). Also called beds.

Brick Clay that is molded to shape and fired at high temperatures in a large kiln or oven. The color of the natural clay determines the color of the brick.

Broom finish The texture created when a concrete surface is stroked with a stiff broom while the concrete is still curing.

Buttering Placing mortar on a masonry unit using a trowel.

Collar joint The vertical joint between wythes.

Concave joint A masonry joint that is recessed and formed in mortar. A curved steel jointing tool is used to make a concave joint.

Concrete Fresh concrete is a semifluid mixture of portland cement, sand (fine aggregate), gravel, or crushed stone.

Concrete block A masonry unit that consists of an outside shell with a hollow center that is divided by two or three vertical webs. The ends of the unit may have flanges that accept mortar and join with adjacent blocks, or they may have smooth ends for corners and the ends of walls.

Concrete pavers Commonly used for patios and walks, concrete pavers come in a number of shapes and colors and are designed to be laid in a sand base without mortar; some interlock to form repeating patterns.

Control joints Special joints, also called contraction joints, that are tooled into the surface and make concrete crack in straight lines at planned locations.

Curing The process by which concrete becomes solid and develops strength. Proper moisture reduces cracking and shrinkage.

Darby A long tool used for smoothing the surface of a concrete slab.

Edging joints The rounded edges of a pour that are resistant to cracking.

Excavation To dig out earth or soil so that a slab will be supported by a subgrade that is hard, uniformly graded, and well drained.

Expansion joint A planned break in the continuous surface of a structure into which a compressible material has been placed. The material absorbs pressure when the surface expands when heated. This joint prevents buckling or crumbling of the surface. Expansion joints are required wherever dissimilar materials adjoin because they will expand and contract at different rates.

Face brick A type of brick used when consistency in appearance is required. A batch of face brick will be quite uniform in color, size, texture, and face structure.

Flagstone pattern "Carving" a design into concrete to create a pattern.

Floating The process of smoothing the surface of a pour with a float made of steel, aluminum, magnesium, or wood. This action drives large aggregate below the surface.

Footing Support for garden walls of brick, block, or stone. Generally made of concrete, footings are also used for stairs and are usually located below the local frost line to avoid problems from frost heave.

Formwork The forms or molds that contain and shape wet concrete. Forms are usually built from lumber; plywood is used for curved sections.

Frost heave Shifting or upheaval of the ground resulting from alternate freezing and thawing of water in the soil.

Frost line The maximum depth to which soil freezes in the winter. The local building department can provide information of the frost-line depth in your area.

Header The brick position in a wall in which the brick is rotated 90° from the stretcher position so that the end is facing out.

Hydration The process of cement particles chemically reacting with water. When this happens the concrete hardens into a durable material.

Mason's line A length of twine that is held at each end by an L-shaped block. The line can be stretched tight and is used as a straightedge guide, permitting the mason to check the evenness of the course being laid.

Mortar A mixture of cementitious materials, fine aggregate, and water. Mortar is used to bond bricks or blocks.

Nominal dimensions The dimensions of a masonry unit plus one mortar joint.

Portland cement A mixture of burned lime, iron, silica, and alumina. This mixture is put through a kiln, then ground into a fine powder and packaged for sale. The cement is the same color as the gray limestone quarried near Portland, England.

Prepackaged concrete mix A mix that combines cement, sand, and gravel in the correct proportions and requires only the addition of water to create fresh concrete.

Ready-mix concrete Wet concrete that is transported from a concrete supplier. The concrete is ready to pour.

Rebar Reinforcing bar (called rebar for short), is used for concrete that will carry a heavy load, such as footings, foundation walls, columns, and pilasters.

Reinforcing mesh Steel wires woven or welded into a grid of 6 or 10 inch squares. The mesh is primarily used in flatwork, such as walks and patios.

Retaining walls A wall built to hold back a slope. Retaining walls are used to create terraces in sloping ground.

Rowlock A brick laid on its face edge horizontally so that the face is visible in the wall.

Sailor A brick laid on its end vertically so that the end is visible in the wall.

Screeding Using a straight 2x4 moved from one end of a concrete pour to the other to strike off excess concrete and level the surface.

Segregation A condition that results when the concrete is overworked—such as when trying to remove air bubbles—and the water separates and rises to the top.

Soap A brick that is halved in width.

Soldier A brick standing upright with the edge facing out.

Split A brick that is halved in height.

Steel reinforcement Reinforcing mesh or rebar that is used to strengthen concrete.

Stretcher A brick that is laid lengthwise in the course.

Stucco A cementitious material made of sand, portland cement, lime, and water. Stucco is applied in thin layers to provide a durable finish for walls.

Troweling Finishing the concrete after it has been screeded. This finishing step is for interior concrete applications and concrete without air-entrainment.

Weep hole A hole in a retaining wall that allows water to seep through.

Wythe The vertical section of a wall that is equal to the width of the masonry unit.

Index

Index

SOURCES

PHOTOGRAPHERS:
Brian Vanden Brink, Rockport, ME; 207-236-4035. Donna H. Chiarelli, Kutztown, PA; 610-683-7574. Betty Crowell, Montecito, CA; 805-969-8218. Alan & Linda Detrick, Glen Rock, NJ; 201-444-6466. Ken Druse, Brooklyn, NY; 718-230-0184. Phillip H. Ennis, Bedford, NY; 914-234-9574. Ivy D Photography, Inc., North Babylon, NY; 631-254-0761. Richard Felber, New York, NY; 212-242-5426. The Garden Picture Library, London, UK; +44 020 7228 4332. Tony Giammarino, Richmond, VA; 804-320-9709. Anne Gummerson, Baltimore, MD; 410-276-6936. Charles Mann, Santa Fe, NM; 505-474-3180. Jerry Pavia, Bonners Ferry, ID; 208-267-7374. Positive Images, Haverhill, MA; 978-556-9366. Red Cover, London, UK; +44 020 7751 0110. Michael S. Thompson, Eugene, OR; 541-485-0805. Jessie Walker, Glencoe, IL; 847-835-0522.

DESIGNERS & ARCHITECTS:
Roc Caivano, Architect, Bar Harbor, ME. Cording Landscape Design, Inc., Towaco, NJ. Christine Doctor/The Plant Doctor, Inc., Glen Cove, NY. Ellis Lan Design, Atlanta, GA. Garden Designs, Richmond, VA. Mark Hutker & Assoc., Architects, Vineyard Haven, MA. Horiuchi & Solien, Landscape Architects, Falmouth, MA. Melville Thomas Architects, Baltimore, MD. Rose Gardens by Michael, Ridgefield Park, NJ. Sarah Schweizer, Architect, Monkton, MD. Weatherend Estate Furniture, Rockland, ME. Sam Williamson, Landscape Architect, Portland, OR.

Photo Credits

Front Cover: Todd Caverly, Photographer/Brian Vanden Brink Photos, designer: George Snead, Jr. **page 1:** Richard Felber **page 2:** Jessie Walker **page 8:** Tony Giammarino, designer: Garden Designs/Carrington Brown **pages 10-11:** Richard Felber **page 12:** *top* Alan & Linda Detrick, designer: Cording Landscape Design, Inc.; *bottom right* Anne Gummerson; *bottom left* Derek Fell **page 13:** *top* Hugh Palmer/Red Cover; *bottom right* Jerry Pavia; *bottom left* Phillip H. Ennis, designer: Stephen Krog **page 14:** *top right* Alan & Linda Detrick, designer: Cording Landscape Design, Inc.; *bottom right and bottom left* Jerry Pavia; *top left* Brian Vanden Brink, landscape architects: Horiuchi & Solien **page 15:** *top* Alan & Linda Detrick; *center* Jerry Pavia, *bottom* Anne Gummerson **page 16:** Richard Felber **page 18:** Michael S. Thompson, garden by: Richard Bray **page 19:** *top* Brian Vanden Brink, landscape architects: Horiuchi & Solien; *bottom* Jerry Pavia **page 20:** Brian Vanden Brink, landscape architects: Horiuchi & Solien **page 21:** *left* Phillip H. Ennis, designers: Steve Godwin & Rod Pleasant; *right* Brian Vanden Brink, landscape architects: Horiuchi & Solien **page 22:** Jerry Pavia **page 23:** *both* Alan & Linda Detrick, bottom designer: Cording Landscape Design, Inc. **page 24:** Phillip H. Ennis, designers: Steve Godwin & Rod Pleasant **page 25:** Brian Vanden Brink, landscape architects: Horiuchi & Solien **pages 26-27:** *all* John Parsekian **page 28:** Brian Vanden Brink, architects: Mark Hutker & Assoc. **page 29:** Todd Caverly, Photographer/Brian Vanden Brink Photos, designer: George Snead, Jr. **page 30:** *both* Brian Vanden Brink, top designer: Harbor Farm; bottom architects: Mark Hutker & Assoc. **page 31:** *top* Howard Rice/Garden Picture Library; *bottom* Alan & Linda Detrick, designer: The New York Botanical Gardens **page 32:** *top* Ken Druse; *bottom* Anne Gummerson, architect: Sarah Schweizer **page 33:** *top* Steven Wooster/Garden Picture Library; *bottom* Brian Vanden Brink, designer: Io Oakes **pages 34 & 37:** Brian Vanden Brink, page 34 architect: Sam Van Dam, page 37 architect: Rob Whitten **pages 38-39:** Alan & Linda Detrick,

bottom designer: Cording Landscape Design, Inc. **page 40:** Phillip H. Ennis, designer: Bill Shanahan **page 41:** Lee Anne White/Positive Images, designer: Ellis Lan Design **page 42:** Ken Druse **page 43:** *both* Alan & Linda Detrick, designer: Cording Landscape Design, Inc. **pages 44-45:** *both* Brian Vanden Brink, page 44 designer: Weatherend Estate Furniture, page 45 architect: Sally Weston **pages 48-50:** *all* Jessie Walker, page 50 top landscape architect: Doug Moerre **page 51:** *top row* Michael S. Thompson, designers: Sarah & Lance Robertson; *bottom* Jessie Walker **page 52:** *left* Brian Vanden Brink, architects: Scholz & Barclay; *right* Jerry Pavia **page 53:** *top left* Hugh Palmer/Red Cover; *top right* Brian C. Nieves/CH; *bottom* Michael S. Thompson, designer: Marietta & Ernie O'Byrne **page 54:** Jessie Walker **page 56:** J.S. Sira/Garden Picture Library **page 57:** Mark Lohman **page 58:** Michael S. Thompson, designer: Elizabeth Lair **page 59:** Jessie Walker, designer: Doug Moerre **page 60:** *top* Jerry Howard/Positive Images; *bottom* Karen Bussolini/Positive Images, designer: Site Design Assoc. **page 61:** Lee Anne White/Positive Images **pages 62-63:** *center* Alan & Linda Detrick; *right* Donna H. Chiarelli/CH **page 64:** Ken Druse **pages 66-67:** Jerry Howard/Positive Images, designer: Tom Wirth **page 73:** John Parsekian/CH **pages 74, 76, & 77:** *all* Jessie Walker **page 78:** *both* Charles Mann **page 79:** John Parsekian/CH **page 80:** *top left* Eric Crichton/Garden Picture Library; top right Clive Nichols/Garden Picture Library **page 81:** Alan & Linda Detrick, designer: The New York Botanical Gardens **page 82:** Brian C. Nieves/CH **page 83:** Brigette Thomas/Garden Picture Library **page 84:** Alan & Linda Detrick, designer: Cording Landscape Design, Inc. **page 85:** Karen Bussolini/Positive Images **page 86:** Richard Felber **pages 89:** *all* Merle Henkenius **pages 90, 91, & 92:** *all* John Parsekian/CH **pages 94-95:** *top center* Ivy Moriber Neal/Ivy D Photography, Inc., designer: Christine Doctor/The Plant Doctor; *top right* Ken Druse; *bottom right* Donna H. Chiarelli/CH; *bottom center right & bottom center left* Alan & Linda Detrick; *bottom*

left Hugh Palmer/Red Cover **page 96:** *top* Phillip H. Ennis; *bottom* courtesy of Bomanite **page 97:** *top left* Brian C. Nieves/CH; *top right* Jerry Pavia; *bottom* Richard Felber **page 98:** Jessie Walker **page 100:** Tony Giammarino, designers: Annabelle & John Josephs **page 101:** Anne Gummerson, architect: Sarah Schweizer **page 102:** John Parsekian/CH **page 103:** John Parsekian **page 104:** Merle Henkenius **page 108:** *all* John Parsekian/CH **pages 110-111:** *top left* Jessie Walker; *top right and bottom row* John Parsekian/CH **pages 112-113:** *top left* John Parsekian/CH; *top right* Charles Mann; *bottom row* John Parsekian/CH **page 116:** Betty Crowell **page 118:** Anne Gummerson **page 120:** *top* Charles Mann; *bottom* Alan & Linda Detrick, designer: Rose Gardens by Michael **page 129:** courtesy of Bomanite **pages 132-133:** Richard Felber **page 134:** *top* Brian Vanden Brink, designer: Weatherend Estate Furniture; *bottom right* James M. Mejuto; *bottom left* Karen Bussolini **page 135:** *top left* Charles Mann; *top right* Derek Fell; *bottom* Brian C. Nieves/CH **pages 136-137:** *top left* Mark Bolton/Red Cover; *top center* John Schwartz, *center* Crandall & Crandall *top right* Brian C. Nieves/CH; *bottom right* Terry Wild Studio; *bottom center right* Brian Vanden Brink, architects: Robinson & Grisaru; *bottom center left* Patricia J. Bruno/Positive Images; *bottom left* Charles Mann **page 138:** John Parsekian **page 141:** *top* Brian Vanden Brink, landscape architects: Horiuchi & Solien; *bottom row* John Parsekian/CH **page 142:** Brian Vanden Brink, architects: Mark Hutker and Assoc. **pages 143-145:** John Parsekian/CH **page 146:** Derek Fell **page 153:** John Parsekian/CH **pages 154-155:** *top left* Betty Crowell; *top right both* Brian C. Nieves/CH; *center and bottom rows* John Parsekian/CH **page 156:** Anne Gummerson, architects: Melville Thomas Architects **page 159:** *both* Derek Fell **pages 160-163:** *all* John Parsekian/CH **page 164:** *both* Brian Vanden Brink, top landscape architects: Horiuchi & Solien, bottom designer: Ron Forest Fences **page 165:** *top* Brian Vanden Brink, landscape architects: Horiuchi & Solien; *bottom right* Betty Crowell; *bot-*

tom left Alan & Linda Detrick **page 166:** *top* Brian Vanden Brink, architects: Mark Hutker and Assoc.; *bottom row* Jerry Pavia **page 167:** *top & center* Alan & Linda Detrick; *bottom* Charles Mann **page 168:** Grey Crawford/Red Cover **pages 171, 173-181:** *all* John Parsekian/CH **page 182:** Jessie Walker **page 185:** Tony Giammarino **page 196:** Brian Vanden Brink, architects: Mark Hutker and Assoc. **page 198:** Tony Giammarino, designer: Keystone Retaining Wall Systems **page 199:** Alan & Linda Detrick **pages 202-204:** John Parsekian/CH **pages 206-207:** Todd Caverly, Photographer/ Brian Vanden Brink Photos, designer: George Snead, Jr. **page 208:** *top left* Anne Gummerson; *top right* Alan & Linda Detrick, designer: Cording Landscape Design, Inc.; *bottom right* Richard Felber; *bottom left* Brian Vanden Brink, designer: Roc Caivano **page 209:** *top* courtesy of Interlocking Concrete Pavement Institute; *bottom right* Alan & Linda Detrick; *bottom left* Jerry Pavia **page 210:** *top right* Alan & Linda Detrick, designer: Cording Landscape Design, Inc.; *bottom right* Sunniva Harte/Garden Picture Library; *bottom left* Andreas von Einsiedel/Red Cover; *center left* Ron Sutherland/Garden Picture Library; *top left* Brian Vanden Brink, designer: Weatherend Estate Furniture **page 211:** Brian Vanden Brink, designer: Weatherend Estate Furniture **pages 212-213:** Karen Bussolini/Positive Images, designer: Johnsen Landscapes and Pools **pages 214-215:** *left and center* Alan & Linda Detrick; *right* Jerry Pavia **page 216:** Jessie Walker **pages 217-219:** Brian C. Nieves/CH **pages 220-221:** Ron Sutherland/Garden Picture Library **page 222:** Jessie Walker **page 223-226** *all* John Parsekian/CH **page 227:** *top* courtesy of Bomanite; *center & bottom* courtesy of Artcrete **page 228:** *top left* Brian Vanden Brink, landscape architect: Sam Williamson; *top right* Jerry Pavia **page 229-231** *all* John Parsekian/CH

Have a home improvement, decorating, or gardening project? Look for these and other fine **Creative Homeowner books** wherever books are sold.

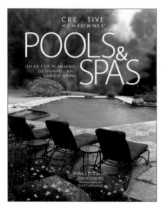

Learn everything about pools, from planning to installation. 300 color photos. 224 pp.; 8½"×10⅞"
BOOK #: 277853

Step-by-step deck building for the novice. 500+ color photos, illustrations. 192 pp.; 8½"×10⅞"
BOOK #: 277162

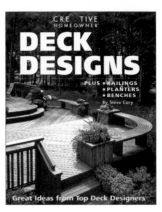

Plans from top deck designer-builders. 300+ color photos, illustrations. 192 pp.; 8½"×10⅞"
BOOK #: 277369

Design ideas, planning advice, and projects. 460+ color photos, illustrations. 160 pp; 8½"×10⅞"
BOOK #: 274804

How to build 20 furniture projects. 470+ color photos, illustrations. 208 pp.; 8½"×10⅞"
BOOK #: 277462

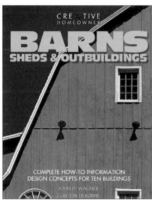

Plan, construct, and finish outbuildings. 600+ color photos, illustrations. 208 pp.; 8½"×10⅞"
BOOK #: 277818

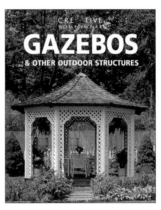

Designing, building techniques for yard structures. 450+ color photos, illustrations. 160 pp.; 8½"×10⅞"
BOOK #: 277138

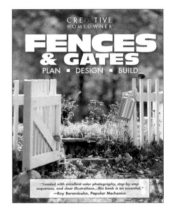

Includes step-by-step instructions for building fences. 400 color photos. 144 pp.; 8½"×10⅞"
BOOK #: 277985

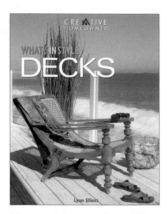

Newest designs, products. 200+ color photos. 128 pp.; 8½"×10⅞"
BOOK #: 277183

Design your own deck. 250+ color photos. 128 pp.; 8½"×10⅞"
BOOK #: 277155

Impressive guide to garden design and plant selection. 600+ color photos, illustrations. 320 pp.; 9"×10"
BOOK #: 274615

Lavishly illustrated with portraits of over 100 flowering plants; 500+ color photos. 208 pp.; 9"×10"
BOOK #: 274032